The
DRIP
Strategy

The
DRIP
Strategy

Building Your Wealth
One Share at a Time with
Dividend Reinvestment Plans

Michael B. Decter

Published in 2001 by Stoddart Publishing Co. Limited
895 Don Mills Road, 400-2 Park Centre, Toronto, Canada M3C 1W3
180 Varick Street, 9th Floor, New York, New York 10014

Distributed by:
General Distribution Services Ltd.
325 Humber College Blvd., Toronto, Ontario M9W 7C3
Tel. (416) 213-1919   Fax (416) 213-1917
Email cservice@genpub.com

05 04 03 02 01 1 2 3 4 5

Canadian Cataloguing in Publication Data

Decter, Michael B.
The drip strategy : building your wealth one share at a time
with dividend reinvestment plans

Includes index.
ISBN 0-7737-6119-5

1. Dividend reinvestment. I. Title.

HG5152.D43 2001   332.63'22   C00-932832-7

Every reasonable effort has been made to contact the holders
of copyright for materials quoted in the book. The author and publisher
will gladly receive information that will enable them to rectify any
inadvertent errors or omissions in subsequent editions.

Cover design: Bill Douglas @ The Bang
Text design: Joseph Gisini/PageWave Graphics Inc.
Page composition: Kevin Cockburn/PageWave Graphics Inc.

The Canada Council | Le Conseil des Arts
FOR THE ARTS | DU CANADA
SINCE 1957 | DEPUIS 1957

*We acknowledge for their financial support of our publishing program the Canada
Council, the Ontario Arts Council, and the Government of Canada
through the Book Publishing Industry Development Program (BPIDP).*

Printed and bound in Canada

For my children,
Riel and Geneviève

Contents

Acknowledgements. ix

Introduction
One Share at a Time 1

Chapter 1
DRIPs 101: What Is a DRIP and Why Should You Care?. 5

Chapter 2
Getting Rich Slowly: Putting the DRIP Strategy to Work 15

Chapter 3
Getting Started: Open Your First DRIP Today!. 27

Chapter 4
Investment Tradecraft: Be Your Own Investment Advisor 37

Chapter 5
The True North: My Favourite Canadian DRIPs 51

Chapter 6
Land of Opportunity: My Favourite American DRIPs 85

Chapter 7
Useful Resources for the DRIP Investor 113

Chapter 8
More DRIPs to Investigate 123

Chapter 9
DRIPs for My Kids and Yours. 147

Concluding Thoughts. 153

Appendix: More International DRIPs 155

Useful Terms to Know. 169

Index. 173

Acknowledgements

MY THANKS TO ROBERT MACKWOOD, MY TIRELESS AGENT, AND TO Perry Goldsmith, the thoughtful and determined founder and president of Contemporary Communications, for finding a home for these stories. The team at Stoddart have once again proven to be a pleasure to work with, in particular, Jack Stoddart, Marnie Kramarich, Angel Guerra, and Don Bastian. This is my third book with Stoddart and my respect for this excellent Canadian company continues to grow. Marnie's terrific advice on reordering the manuscript dramatically improved the book. Elizabeth d'Anjou, who has saved me from numbing the reader, came through with wonderful advice on how to shape and reshape the book. Gillian Watts's copy edit aided greatly. Thank you, Marnie, Gillian, and Elizabeth. You all deserve co-author status!

A special thank you to Anna Porter for her selfless and kind advice. They say that, in law, testimony against one's own interest is particularly powerful; Anna's advice fits the description and I remain grateful for it.

I owe a significant debt to David Chilton, a.k.a. the Wealthy Barber. In the early days of thinking about this book, when publishers were less than keen, I sent an outline of the concept to David. I returned to my office one day after lunch, a little dejected, and played my voice-mail messages. The extremely positive message from David lifted my spirits and encouraged me to stay the course and write this book. I am deeply grateful to David Chilton for his enthusiasm. I saved his message and played it on bad days when I needed support. I hope he enjoys this book a fraction as much as I enjoyed his message and his landmark book!

Another David is also owed a debt for his contribution to *The DRIP Strategy*. David Martin and I were close friends through our high-school years. For many of our adult years we lived in different cities and saw each other only occasionally. More recently we reconnected with the elusive goal of recovering the fitness of our youth. As I toiled over this manuscript, David and I swam laps together at a downtown Toronto pool. His own anxieties about financial security in retirement aided this book in reaching its completion. Thank you, David.

My colleagues at Lawrence and Company have been supportive of my efforts, although mystified by why I would subject myself to such additional toil. I am grateful to Jack Lawrence, Tony Pampena, Ravi Sood, Grant McCutcheon, and Michael Giordano. The dynamic duo of Lily Fidelj and Connie de Santos waded in when my desperation showed. They have my gratitude for their good-humoured assistance. A special thanks also to Kim Geddes and Marie (Mary) MacArthur, who helped put these words on paper.

I am also grateful to Pamela Wallin for her encouraging words and support as I struggled to translate ideas into readable words.

My deep appreciation goes to my daughter, Geneviève, who aided in the inputting of the manuscript during our holiday at Lake Joseph in the summer of 1999. It was during our time together at the cottage that the book was transformed into a real conversation.

Introduction
One Share at a Time

THIS BOOK HAS ITS ORIGINS IN MY PREVIOUS INVESTMENT BOOK, *Michael Decter's Million-Dollar Strategy*, which was published by Stoddart in 1998. More accurately, its roots are in the tour to promote that book. *Million-Dollar Strategy* chronicled my adventures building a million-dollar-plus registered retirement savings plan (RRSP) over an 11-year period. (For American readers, an RRSP is a Canadian self-directed pension account much like an IRA or Keogh plan.) When I toured Canada to promote *Million-Dollar Strategy*, one of the most frequently asked questions was "How much money do I need to start investing?"

My answer was in two parts. First, I acknowledged that a $20,000 lump-sum refund of contributions from a pension plan had kick-started my own retirement investing. Then I argued that you could really start with any amount, no matter how small. This answer, however, seemed to lack credibility with the tentative would-be investors. For many of them, $20,000 seemed to be an unobtainable fortune. My impression was that they only heard the number *$20,000*, not my longer, more thoughtful answer. Each time I was asked this question I wished I had a better answer for it.

Upon reflection, I have decided that I do have a better answer, and here it is!

The starting point for this book was my realization that my own investing adventures were not limited to my RRSP, the subject of my previous book. I had also started to invest in a number of dividend reinvestment plans or DRIPs. This strategy has no barrier to entry — you don't need $20,000 or $50,000 or even $1,000. For as little as $25 you can buy one share of any one of literally hundreds of corporations. This single share can be the first tiny step on a road to successful investment. DRIPs and their first cousins, direct purchase plans (DPPs) or share purchase plans (SPPs), are the cornerstone of an investment strategy that every investor, no matter how modest his or her initial capital, can use to succeed. As discussed in this book, many DRIPs incorporate the features of DPPs and SPPs.

But, you may be thinking, don't you need tens or even hundreds of thousands of dollars to play the stock market? Didn't Warren Buffett start with several hundred thousand dollars? How can you seriously invest with only a few dollars? How can you expect a broker to take you seriously when you want to buy shares one at a time? Would not the commissions and paperwork alone be prohibitive? In short, why write (or read) a book that has *One Share at a Time* in the subtitle?

The answer is that "one share at a time" is an excellent investment approach. You do not need a broker to start investing. Nor do you need a fortune, small or large. And most paperwork can be avoided. Using a dividend reinvestment plan, or DRIP, strategy, I genuinely believe that if you are willing to take a first step into investing, you can do it, one step — one share — at a time. *You can succeed.* The modest dollar amount required to start allows you to build an investment portfolio of your own, starting *now*. For $25 or $50 per month, you can begin a journey with the potential to greatly assist your eventual retirement. As your circumstances allow, you can increase the amount of your investment, or reduce it if necessary. This is a path I have travelled with considerable success. In the pages that follow, you will find both the practical tools and the inspiration to do it yourself.

The DRIP Strategy is organized into nine chapters.

In the first part of the book I explain the basics of DRIPs. What are they? How do they work? How do they fit into an investment strategy? Chapters 1 and 2 address these fundamentals, and also treat such topics as the importance of regularity in your contributions and of setting goals. Chapter 3 helps you take the next step, telling you how you can get started — immediately, if you like. Finally, in Chapter 4 I give some advice on how to choose solid companies for your portfolio. My "investment tradecraft" rules — my strategy for selecting good value in stocks — were outlined in my previous book. Here I review them, but also talk about how each relates specifically to DRIP investing, and also discuss how thinking about cultural and economic trends can help you make smart choices. These chapters make up a practical guide to the hows and whys of DRIPs.

Next, I tell the story — or more properly, stories — about building my own DRIP investment portfolio. I discuss my own holdings in both Canada (Chapter 5) and the United States (Chapter 6), giving some background on the companies and some insight into why I chose them — and let you know how the investments have turned out so far. When I started, I had no guide. My hope is that my experiences can serve as lessons for other new DRIP investors.

The following chapters serve as a resource guide. Chapter 7 points you to a host of wonderful tools for DRIP investors, including resources for learning more about companies as potential investments. The best way to get most of this information these days is on the Internet, and I include addresses for a number of useful DRIP Web sites as well as a list of periodicals and books. Chapter 8 supplies lists of solid companies offering DRIPs, above and beyond the ones in my own portfolio. It examines Canadian DRIPs; American offerings, which are much more numerous and often offer good value; and "the foreign legion" — DRIPs offered by companies located outside North America. Finally, Chapter 9 is a brief discussion of DRIP investing and kids, which I think could be a fine mix.

If you are nervous about taking your first step on the investment journey, let this book be your encouragement and your guide. *The DRIP Strategy* offers a low-cost yet powerful entry into the world of share ownership, which is the single best means of securing a better retirement and greater financial security for your future. If you are fortunate enough to have a pension from your employer or a well funded RRSP or Keogh plan, then a DRIP strategy can be an important additional source of retirement security. If you are depending on savings for retirement, then DRIPs can be a great vehicle for maximizing growth of your hard-earned dollars.

Chapter 1

DRIPs 101
What Is a DRIP and
Why Should You Care?

W HILE I WAS WORKING ON THIS BOOK, MY 14-YEAR-OLD daughter, Geneviève, began to ask an endless stream of questions. It was the summer of 1999 and we were vacationing at Lake Joseph, north of Toronto, while I worked fitfully on the manuscript. I decided to include her questions and my answers in the chapters that follow. I hope this approach is helpful to your understanding of DRIP issues.

We were lingering over a hearty Canadian cottage breakfast of peameal bacon, hash browns, and scrambled eggs. My laptop sat precariously between the toast plate and the bowl of oranges. The dual challenges of fatherhood and authorship hovered before me just as awkwardly.

"What are you writing about?" demanded the always-curious Geneviève.

"DRIP investing," I replied.

"What is a DRIP, Papa?" she asked, naturally enough.

"Well, DRIP stands for Dividend ReInvestment Plan. Some companies offer their shareholders the option of using their dividends to buy more shares, rather than receiving them in cash."

"What is a dividend?" inquired Geneviève, and then added, "This is about making money, isn't it?"

"Okay, it is about making money — I admit it," I replied with a laugh. "A dividend is how a company shares its profits with its shareholders. Well-established companies pay regular dividends. For example, every three months the Ford Motor Company currently pays each shareholder a dividend of 28 cents for each share they own. So if I own 10 shares of Ford, I get $2.80 from them four times a year. But if I'm a member of their dividend reinvestment plan, instead of giving it to me, they would use it to buy me more shares — or a part of a share, if my dividend is less than the share price."

"So when do you actually get the money?" asked the ever-skeptical Geneviève.

"Later on, after it has grown, you can get the money in either of two ways. You can sell some or all of the shares, or you can cancel the dividend reinvestment plan and start to get paid the dividends," I replied.

"Bo-ring. I want to buy stuff *now*."

"Geneviève, if you spend it all now, you won't have any money when you are old."

She thought about this. It's hard for the young to really believe they'll *ever* be old!

"How do you get started?" was her next question.

"All you need to do is make a first purchase. You pick one company, or more, and buy your first shares."

"Where do you get information about companies? Who do you call to set up a DRIP?" were Geneviève's new questions.

My answer to both was the same: "On the Internet, usually."

Geneviève is an Internet wiz. She demanded, "You mean there are Web sites where you can buy shares?"

"Yes, there are Web sites where you can register directly with companies to buy shares," I replied. "Or you can join an association that helps you buy them."

"Cool!" was her final answer.

My toast was cold by this point, but answering Geneviève's questions had turned my thoughts back to my own first DRIP shares, and helped me focus on the basics for this first chapter.

THE DRIP INVESTMENT STRATEGY

A confession is required at this point. I did not myself get involved in DRIPs as an investment strategy. My first DRIP investments were made solely for the purpose of obtaining annual reports. Owning one share got me on the mailing list for annual reports, quarterly reports, and other company information. My DRIP participation in the pre-Internet era was simply an inexpensive research plan. (Now I can receive annual and quarterly reports through Yahoo! or from company Web sites.) But, after I began to receive monthly statements, I realized that I could easily, cheaply, and regularly add to my holdings of each company. I soon became a serious DRIP investor.

Owning one share of a corporation gives you most of the same rights and privileges as someone who owns a million shares. You have the right to attend the annual meeting and to vote for the board of directors. You are also entitled to receive the annual report to shareholders and, if you wish, the quarterly reports. With a DRIP you also have the right to invest more money, through both dividend reinvestment and direct investment, sometimes without fees or commissions. Your dividends are invested automatically so that your stake in the company grows every time a dividend is issued. Most companies issue dividends quarterly, so every three months your investment increases a little as the dividends buy you additional shares.

My overall investing philosophy is basically the same for DRIPs as it is for other investments. The approach outlined in this book builds upon the thinking outlined in my earlier book, *Michael Decter's Million-Dollar Strategy*. Investing in DRIPs is a portfolio-building technique that allows would-be investors with small amounts of savings to begin investing. It does not replace sound thinking about which companies to select, of course. Rather, it provides a way for you to build your own portfolio of investments in companies — one share at a time.

Nor is a DRIP portfolio a replacement for other forms of

retirement savings. Most of us will depend on several sources of retirement income. Pensions and retirement savings plans, both registered and non-registered, are important components of a retirement strategy. DRIPs are a complementary element. But, as part of a diversified retirement plan, DRIP investing can be a profitable, educational, and fun way for *anyone* to invest, on any scale.

The essential element for success with the DRIP strategy is simply for you to begin. No one can do that for you. It's easy to do — all of the materials you need to enrol in hundreds of DRIPs are available through a single Internet site, DRIP Central, or you can write directly to the companies. For the price of a single stamp or a few minutes on-line, you can embark on your own DRIP investment journey. Having begun, you need to keep on, a little at a time, until all those reinvested dividends and small cheques add up to a sizable portfolio. In only seven years of DRIP investing, I have built two portfolios worth over $200,000 in total.

KEY BENEFITS OF DRIP INVESTING

DRIPs are relatively new vehicles. It is only within the last decade that the U.S. Securities and Exchange Commission (SEC) promulgated Form S-3 for the formation of DRIPs. The S-3 registration statement is the form a company files with the SEC to start a DRIP. The cost of this convenient means for shareholders to invest in their corporation is minimal to the company and constitutes a very progressive innovation important to the economy, since it assists companies in capital formation. DRIPs have other benefits, as well. They allow the board of a corporation to adopt maximum dividend payout policies and still, through shareholder reinvestment, provide capital for corporate growth, since the dividends of DRIP holders will go right back into more shares.

Why invest in DRIPs? What are the benefits of this particular approach to building your retirement security? There are several distinct advantages to DRIP investing, starting with the ability to start small and keep costs low. Several other factors also make

DRIPs an attractive option for the small investor. Let's look at each of the advantages in a little more detail.

Starting Small

The low-cost entry point is perhaps the most important strength of the DRIP approach. Many would-be investors are intimidated by their belief that you need thousands or even tens of thousands of dollars to start investing. Traditional brokerage firms are indeed not eager to attract small investor accounts, which are not very profitable for them. With DRIPs you can substitute your time, as a form of "sweat equity," for the large initial investment that you don't have.

You can begin a DRIP portfolio with as little as $100, and $25 per month lets you continue. Don't be intimidated by Wall Street and the "big money" aura of financial institutions. Many of the American and foreign plans have $250 or $500 minimum initial investments, but will let you pay $50 per month for 5 or 10 months to start.

Low Fees

Low fees, or even no fees, characterize many DRIP plans. Over the past few years some DRIP plans have implemented a range of fees for some transactions, but most DRIPs are still "fee free" for the reinvestment of dividends. Fees are often levied for additional contributions, and sometimes for initial set-up and for withdrawal from the plan. But the fee schedule is often much more affordable than minimum broker's fees, especially for small investments.

Regularity and Discipline

The regular investment of your dividends creates a basic discipline: automatic saving. I encourage you to develop a further investment discipline through automatic bank deductions or regular writing of cheques. There are many famous ways of expressing this advice — "pay yourself first" is one example. To succeed at investing, the bottom line is that you must actually invest. It's easier to do this if you do it in small, regular amounts, especially at first, and a DRIP portfolio is the perfect vehicle for doing this.

The DRIP approach guarantees regular investment by channelling all of your dividends towards the purchase of additional shares. This is a good start to regular investing, but only a start. You also need to put aside dollars each week or each month so that you develop the discipline of investing. Once investing becomes a habit, you are on your way. You may find, as I did, that it becomes a very satisfying habit — and a far less dangerous addiction than tobacco. In fact, if you were to give up smoking and invest the resulting savings in a DRIP portfolio, you would live longer *and* be able to afford your retirement. Giving up other addictions for an investing passion may be one route to finding the cash. Another approach may be to dedicate a small percentage of your income or part of your tax refund to investments. There are many sources for the small amounts you need to get started. Once the statements from your DRIP investments begin arriving, they will help spur you on to add further money.

Automatic Dollar-Cost Averaging

Dollar-cost averaging is a solid principle for investing. By purchasing shares little by little over time rather than all at once, you average the cost of acquiring those shares. So if you buy some shares in company X at $25 each in October, then some at $20 in January, and a few more at $30 in April, your overall cost will be an average of those prices.

DRIP investing achieves automatic dollar-cost averaging because your shares are purchased through regular reinvestment of dividends. Any periodic additional cash investments you make also have the characteristic of dollar-cost averaging. This feature of DRIP investing allows you to build a holding at a generally better average cost, with less risk, than investing all at once.

Stable Company Bias

The very nature of DRIPs produces a bias towards larger, more stable companies, since these are the companies able to pay dividends. Just as the notorious Willie Sutton robbed banks "'cause that's where the money was," investing in DRIPs takes your investment dollars where the money is. Big, stable companies generally have the resources to weather bad times in the economy. Small companies rarely offer DRIPs because those companies pay no dividends. The exception is some technology companies; in certain cases these are worth considering for your DRIP portfolio.

In DRIP investing, you will not go for a roller-coaster ride with newly minted Internet companies or fall for the lure of gold-mine speculation. You will be safe from the next Bre-X fiasco. Of course, not all large companies with DRIPs are immune from financial peril; witness Royal Trust in Canada or Chrysler in the United States. But your risk of real disaster is lower with DRIPs — and if it does come, you may get an early warning when dividends are cancelled or earnings plummet. Time to head for the exit.

DRAWBACKS OF DRIP INVESTING

No investment plan is without flaws or inconveniences, of course. Enthusiastic as I am about DRIPs, I think it only fair to outline a few caveats.

Need for Careful Record Keeping

One legitimate criticism of DRIPs is the amount of record keeping involved. There are, luckily, several ways to help lessen this hassle.

Since there is no such thing as a consolidated statement in the DRIP world, if you invest in 10 different DRIPs you will receive 10 statements, either monthly or quarterly. Fortunately, most DRIPs now offer a year-end statement, so you only absolutely need to hold on to that one statement per plan per year.

My strong advice, however, is to keep *all* statements in an orderly file. If you don't hold on to these statements, you may have difficulty come tax time if you have sold shares and have to determine your cost basis. (And even if you don't decide to sell your shares, you can sometimes be forced to if a merger or takeover results in the cancellation of a DRIP. For more on mergers and on DRIPs and taxes in general, see Chapter 2.)

Of course you need to track every investment you make, whether you buy it via a broker, a mutual fund, or a DRIP. But the small amounts in DRIP investments can mean more paperwork per dollar invested. If the dog eats your investment homework, transfer agents (the entities that administer DRIPs on behalf of the companies) are a good source for replacing your DRIP records. But they are likely to charge you a fee for remedying Fido's handiwork.

With the availability of computers and financial software these days, your record-keeping task is less of a hassle than it once was. Many people use Quicken, for example, to keep track of their DRIP records. I use Yahoo! Finance (more on this in Chapter 7). The Yahoo! portfolio service is easy to use; it is also free. Furthermore, some companies now offer electronic quarterly reports. So DRIP record keeping has never been easier.

Another way to help keep your records hassles to a minimum is to ensure that, when you do sell DRIP shares, you sell all of the shares in one plan.

Loss of Control over Price

When you use DRIPs, you lose precise control over the price at which you buy and sell shares, because your purchases are made automatically on dividend dates. This is the flip side of dollar-cost averaging. Many DRIPs are improving the frequency of buy and sell opportunities in their plans, with several now offering daily buys and sells. Still, you can't match the control that you can get from a broker. DRIPs are best suited for long-term investment; over the long haul, the convenience and low fees make up for this loss of price control. However, if your investment strategies require precise buy and sell prices, then DRIPs are not for you.

IS DRIP INVESTING FOR YOU?

What kind of investor should be using DRIP programs? As the discussion of price control above should make clear, DRIPs are at the far end of the spectrum from day trading. Anyone looking for a big win on the market overnight is not a DRIP-style investor. (On the other hand, day traders who have lost their money and are seeking a better idea should perhaps try DRIP investing instead!)

DRIPs were started with the small, long-term investor in mind. If you are investing $5,000 or $10,000 at a time, the low-cost on-line brokers may make more sense for you. To get those low on-line brokerage commissions, you may have to pony up $1,000 to $15,000 to open an account. If, however, $50 or $500 pay-as-you-go investments are more suitable for your budget, and if your goal is to build a secure retirement little by little over the long run, why not start a DRIP portfolio today?

The next chapter takes a more in-depth look at managing a DRIP portfolio: the key features that distinguish one plan from another; the question of the importance of diversification; the implications of mergers and takeovers; and some tax issues. If you have been intrigued by this first taste of the world of DRIP investing, read on!

Chapter 2

Getting Rich Slowly
Putting the DRIP Strategy to Work

Mʏ CONVERSATION WITH GENEVIÈVE CONTINUED LATER IN THE day, on the dock. We were frequently interrupted by the noise of some overpowered, *Miami Vice*–type powerboats that seemed highly out of place in the peaceful woods of Muskoka. Although, to be fair, I was preparing to tow Geneviève around Lake Joseph on an inner tube with a rented powerboat, albeit a much more modest one.

"So, what do you do after you start all these DRIP plans, Papa?" she asked as we were getting the boat ready.

"The idea is to put a little money into each plan on a regular basis," I replied. "Twenty or fifty dollars every month is the way to a solid investment."

"How will that ever amount to anything?" asked Geneviève dubiously.

"Little bits add up if you keep putting money in," I maintained. "For example, if you bought one share in a DRIP each month for $25 and the share price went up 15 percent per year, in 10 years, depending on the dividends the company paid, you could have as many as 100 shares — worth $10,000."

The figure *$10,000* seemed to get Geneviève's attention, so I continued, "Let me give you a real example. McDonald's is your main burger place, so I decided to invest in its DRIP several years ago — after all, we spend so much money there! I bought one share in 1995, and over the years, little by little, I bought a total of 79 shares. They cost me $3,900 all together. But with stock splits and reinvested dividends, I now own 159 shares, worth about $8,000. That's more than double my investment in about five years."

"Wow! Was McDonald's your best DRIP ever?" inquired my teen angel.

"No, Nortel did even better. I bought 41 shares over five years for a total of $1,430. After a stock split, a spinoff from BCE, and dividends, I now own 244 shares of Nortel, worth over $17,000."

"What's a stock split?" demanded Geneviève next.

"A stock split is when a company gives you more shares for the ones you already own. Often it is a two-for-one split. Say each share of company X was worth $120. The company might split them into twice as many shares worth $60 each. They would give you two of the new shares for every one of the old shares you owned. Companies often split their stock when its price gets over $100 per share. Sometimes the splits are three-for-one or three-for-two."

"When could I spend the money?" was her rapid, 14-year-old response.

"You need to be patient," was all her father could properly respond. "DRIPs are part of a long-term investment strategy."

"What do you mean by a strategy, Papa?"

I tried to avoid the usual jargon. "Basically, a plan," I declared. "A strategy is a plan with some smarts or cleverness to it. A strategy charts a course of action, taking account of events going on around you."

"What events?" inquired Geneviève.

"Well, an investment strategy can be affected by anything important going on in the economy or in the stock markets, or with the industry of the companies you invest in. Mergers and takeovers are one factor," I offered. "So are changing technologies."

"Let's go tubing, el lardo," was her retort as she tossed the tube into the boat. (I took this to be a term of endearment, although the modest, natural tube about my waist rendered it within the bounds of fair comment.)

SLOWLY BUT SURELY

Most diets and exercise programs seem to feature claims of easy effort, such as "only eight minutes a day!" My own, previous investment book proposed a 30-minute-per-morning regimen for success. DRIP investing is like working out: You do it a little bit at a time, but consistently.

The most important element to successful DRIP investing is steady investment. Regularity, not brilliant stock picking, is the path to success. David Chilton's excellent book *The Wealthy Barber* proposes that you "pay yourself first," that is, save before spending. This is simple but sound advice. Investing some of those regular savings by using the DRIP strategy of small but steady, regular investments, with the dividends automatically reinvested, can get you to a much stronger financial position in the long run.

KEY FEATURES OF A DRIP

You know from Chapter 1 what a DRIP is, basically. But the specifics of plans can vary quite a bit from one company to another, and can make a big difference to their cost, convenience, and attractiveness to a small investor.

Key features of DRIPs include how shares are acquired, whether fees are charged or not, whether you have the option of additional cash investments, and, if so, if they can be made through automatic withdrawals from your bank account. Another feature available in some cases is a 5-percent discount on shares purchased through a DRIP. When choosing DRIPs, be most concerned about fees on regular investments and on dividend reinvestment, as they reduce growth potential.

I began to learn about these DRIP features largely through trial and error. I had no guide to DRIP investing when I started this adventure. To help you avoid my mistakes, let's consider each of these features in turn.

Open-Market Purchase versus New Issue

There are two basic types of DRIPs. One type involves purchasing shares in the open market for the accounts of shareholders who are reinvesting their dividends. This type of plan requires the involvement of an outside trustee, either a bank or trust company. The company being invested in does not issue any new shares, meaning that the shareholders reinvest their cash dividends through the trustee, who purchases shares on the open market. In the second type of DRIP, the company issues new shares directly to investors in return for the cash dividends, so no bank or trust company is needed as an intermediary. It shouldn't matter to you as an investor which kind of DRIP a particular company offers, except for one consideration: Fees may be higher in open-market plans.

Dividend-Reinvestment Fee

All plans, of course, feature dividend reinvestment; that's what defines a DRIP, after all. The difference among plans is whether they charge a fee for this basic service. Most do not. If you are interested in a DRIP that does charge a dividend-reinvestment fee, be sure to take that cost into account when you consider the profitability of the investment.

Practice varies widely among companies. In reviewing my most recent DRIP statements, I noticed that McDonald's charged me 75 cents to reinvest a $7.77 dividend — not good. On the other hand, Atmos Energy charged me nothing to reinvest a $24.49 dividend, and neither did ITT Industries to reinvest a $14.96 dividend.

Cash Investment Option

The cash investment option is another important DRIP feature that can enhance the speed with which your investment grows. This is your option to put additional cash directly into shares of the company. In some plans this option is available monthly, in others, quarterly. In some DRIPs you can even arrange an automatic deduction from your bank account.

Not all plans offer this feature. Some allow only the reinvestment of dividends, which slows your ability to build a position. Plans offering the cash investment option often set minimum and maximum investment levels. For example, McDonald's allows you to invest a minimum of $100 and a maximum of $250,000 per year. IBM has a $50-per-year minimum and a $250,000-per-year maximum. By contrast, BC Gas has no minimum and a maximum of $20,000 per year.

Fees are often charged for cash investments. Sometimes, these are flat fees; in other plans, charges are levied on a per-share basis. Some DRIPs charge both a flat amount and a per-share fee.

Discounts

Some plans offer a modest discount, usually 5 percent, on the reinvestment of dividends. This discount is an automatic bonus for DRIP participants. There are even a very few companies that extend the discount to optional cash payments. Obviously this is an attractive feature in a plan.

An example of a company offering a discount is TransCanada PipeLines. Canada's largest pipeline utility offers a 5-percent reinvestment discount and a 5.3-percent dividend.

Set-up and Withdrawal Fees

An additional question you should ask about a DRIP before participating in it is whether a fee is charged to set up your account. These fees range from zero to $15, but most fees are in the range of $5 to $10.

The final area where you may encounter fees is upon exiting a plan. Here charges tend to be higher; one can only guess that this is because companies are less interested in pleasing future ex-investors! These fees range from zero to $20, sometimes with additional charges of up to 12 cents per share.

CHOOSING COMPANIES FOR YOUR DRIP PORTFOLIO

As my DRIP investing continued to expand, I began to take a keener interest in the differences among DRIPs described above. These features have the effect of making a particular DRIP more or less attractive than others. In short, not all DRIPs are created equal. Attention to detail is important, particularly regarding fees, which vary greatly among plans. Plan differences aside, however, it is necessary to take into consideration the quality of the company offering the DRIP.

At the end of the day, a DRIP is only as good as the company in which you own the shares. DRIPs are a technique or mechanism for investing — a good one, to be sure, but only if the underlying company succeeds. Obviously a 5-percent discount is a good feature only if you already like the company offering it. Good DRIP features should not cause you to suspend your judgment about the potential of a company. From an investment standpoint, growth of earnings is the most important quality of any company. When you buy a share, you are really buying a stream of future earnings. The quality of the company should come first as a criterion for selection.

Choosing companies in which to place your investments is the central focus of thousands of investment guides, studies, and learned texts (not to mention of my own *Million-Dollar Strategy* book). I will not attempt to replicate that enormous body of work here. In Chapter 4, however, I will offer some general investment "tradecraft" rules and some advice on taking advantage of economic, cultural, and sectoral trends. Then, in Chapters 5 and 6, I'll detail some of my own successes in DRIP investing, explaining some of the better stock picks I made for my own portfolio. My hope is that you can learn from my experience. Later on I'll offer some suggestions of other companies that are good candidates for a DRIP investment, and point you towards resources where you can get further good advice.

So, by the time you finish reading this book, you should feel fairly confident about choosing at least a few DRIP stocks. Selecting

DRIPs is, after all, somewhat easier than selecting stocks in general, because the number of DRIPs available is far smaller than the total number of companies with publicly traded shares.

DIVERSIFICATION

Diversifying your portfolio is another important element of a successful DRIP investment strategy. Placing all your investments in a single company is not recommended. My own portfolio of 44 companies is too large for most investors. Its size is driven by its history; as described in Chapter 1, I bought many single shares in my pre-Internet days simply as a convenient way to get annual reports, and only later developed a true DRIP investment strategy. I would recommend that you select six companies for your portfolio. Try to choose different industries and geographic areas; this will lower your risk of any one company hitting a problem or any one region suffering slow economic growth. Over time you can expand the number of companies in your DRIP portfolio. I would suggest 20 as a maximum for most people, to allow you to follow their progress carefully.

OTHER ASPECTS OF DRIP INVESTING

Two other topics a would-be DRIP investor should be aware of are the effects of mergers, which are becoming increasingly common, and the tax implications of a DRIP.

Merger Mania

One of the realities of investing in this age of merger mania is that several of your long-term investments will be bought or sold. There is little you can do in these circumstances but hope for a continuance of the DRIP in the new entity. Most of the time a painless transition is offered to DRIP shareholders. Sometimes, in fact, especially in certain sectors that are growing rapidly, a merger can significantly increase the value of your shares.

When three telephone companies merged in Atlantic Canada, I received the following letter from Aliant, the successor company to Bruncor, in which I had been a DRIP investor. This one was painless. The key phrase in the letter is " . . . no action is required on your part to become a member of the Aliant DRP." New shares in the new company were issued on the basis of 1.011 shares for each share previously owned — and no paperwork or tax consequences to fuss with.

This is the kind of letter you like to receive when you are a DRIP investor faced with a merger:

> Enclosed is your Dividend Reinvestment Plan (DRP) statement showing the July 16, 1999 reinvestment of your final "Bruncor Inc." dividend, payable July 15, 1999.
>
> All of your Bruncor DRP shares held by the Administrator on your behalf (non-certificated "Plan" shares) were automatically converted to Aliant common shares, effective June 1, 1999. You received 1.011 Aliant shares for every Bruncor share. This conversion is reflected in the "opening balance" figure of your statement.
>
> This statement shows your Bruncor dividend of $0.1625 per share (record date May 20, 1999, payable July 15, 1999), along with any optional cash payments you may have submitted. These funds have been used to purchase common shares of Aliant Inc. The Bruncor dividend is shown in two parts: the dividend earned on your non-certificated "Plan" shares, and the dividend earned on your certificated shares.
>
> As part of our efforts to make the transition to Aliant as seamless and convenient as possible for our shareholders, no action is required on your part to become a member of the Aliant DRP. Your existing Bruncor DRP account has been automatically enrolled in the new Plan. Your Aliant shares (including certificated and non-certificated "Plan" shares), as well as any unexchanged Bruncor certificated shares (if applicable), will continue to participate in the Aliant DRP, unless you request otherwise.

If you hold Bruncor share certificates and have not submitted them for exchange to Aliant shares, please do so at your earliest convenience.

If you have any questions, please call CIBC Mellon Trust at 1-800-565-2188, or call Aliant Investor Relations at 1-877-AIT-3113
Sincerely,

Douglas C. McDade
Director, Investor Relations

Not all mergers are so painless for the DRIP investor. One of my few frustrations with the DRIP strategy is the less seamless kind of corporate takeover. Once in a while — more often than in the past — I receive a letter like the recent one from the CMP Group Inc., which said in part:

The Boards of Directors of CMP Group Inc. and Energy East Corporation have agreed to a merger in which a newly formed, wholly owned subsidiary of Energy East will merge into CMP Group. In exchange for each share of CMP Group common stock, CMP Group shareholders will receive $29.50 in cash, without interest, if the merger is completed.

Financially, I will do extremely well in this takeover. My shares were purchased for less than half the $29.50 takeover price. But the tax and accounting hassles of an involuntarily closed DRIP are a pain; sometimes the tax owed can be difficult to calculate.

Similarly, when the U.S. railway Illinois Central was taken over by Canadian National, the Illinois Central DRIP ended. Taxes were payable on the capital gains and no ongoing participation was offered. This was a disappointment to me; I had to start over and recycle those DRIP investment dollars into another company.

In general, however, most of the mergers I have been affected by in my DRIP investing have allowed a merger of DRIP plans and no tax or disruption. When the Ford Motor Company spun out its parts subsidiary, Visteon, into a separate company, Ford DRIP shareholders were fortunately offered a seamless transfer into a new Visteon DRIP.

If the worst comment about the DRIP strategy is that sometimes takeovers cause you some accounting and tax issues — at the same time as they bring you significant gains — that's not a particularly painful outcome! And it does offer the opportunity to reinvest your gains in other DRIP companies.

DRIPs and Taxes

There are two basic tax issues related to DRIP investments. The first is the annual income tax you owe on dividends. One side effect of the forced savings element of DRIPs is that you pay tax on the dividends each year, even though you have not actually received them as cash. You have, however, received the benefit of owning the additional shares purchased with your dividends. Fortunately for you, dividends are taxed at a lower rate than employment income. If you don't sell any of your DRIP shares, your annual tax hassle consists merely of accounting for the reinvested dividends as ordinary income for tax purposes. Companies make this calculation easy by issuing T-5 forms in Canada or 1099 dividend forms in the United States. You just need to add the dividends to your income.

The second issue is the tax on any capital gains resulting from selling your DRIP shares. As noted above, careful record keeping is essential, especially since a merger or takeover could lead to the cancellation of the DRIP, forcing you to sell your shares at any time. The recently lowered tax on capital gains is now half the rate of tax on employment income. Note that you pay capital gains tax only when you sell.

If you do sell shares, your cost basis for tax purposes is the sum of the following three items: your initial purchase amount, the sum of all reinvested dividends, and the sum of all optional cash payments. Once you have added these three items, subtract the total from your sale proceeds — this is your gain or loss for tax purposes. If you keep your statements, you can obtain the necessary figures easily, but it does require that you diligently store your DRIP records.

If you inherit a DRIP after its owner dies, the cost basis is stepped up upon inheritance. There is no need to piece together the buying history prior to inheritance; you just need to note the inherited value and start there.

GET RICH SLOWLY

Building and managing a DRIP portfolio can be a very simple approach to investing. Regularity is the key. Every month or every quarter you can allocate your new investment dollars — even if they total only $25 or $50 per month — to the companies you believe will perform the best over the long term. When choosing DRIPs, consider the features of the specific plan before investing, especially the fees, but keep the prospects of the actual stock as your primary consideration (Chapter 4 offers advice on investment approaches). Pick several companies in different industries and/or different places to reduce your overall risk. Keep careful records and use them to make tax time less painful. Finally, be ready for a few surprises in the form of mergers or takeovers. Then sit back and watch your investments grow, little by little, over time.

The DRIP strategy is certainly not a get-rich-quick approach. It is the opposite, requiring patience and discipline over a lengthy period of time. It might be best described as the get-rich-slow-but-steady approach. The key point is that the DRIP strategy is a low-risk way to dramatically improve your retirement income through careful savings and investment.

As you will see from reading about some of my own experiences (in Chapters 5 and 6), there is also a very real potential to enjoy terrific returns from some companies. As stodgy telephone utility stocks such as Bell Canada Enterprises (BCE) are rocketed skyward by the digital revolution, you can go along for the ride. In other cases, solid growth over many years produces outstanding returns.

Are you ready to take the next step? Chapter 3 tells you everything you need to know to get started on your own DRIP adventure right away. I'll discuss choosing your first investment, finding the right size for your portfolio, setting up a file for your paperwork, and tracking the progress of your investments. Finally, I'll talk about setting goals that are realistic and workable for you, and provide information about some organizations you can turn to for assistance. When you've finished reading that chapter, you'll have all the tools you need to set up your first DRIP.

Chapter 3

Getting Started
Open Your First DRIP Today!

AFTER I TOWED GENEVIÈVE AROUND LAKE JOSEPH, WE RETURNED to the dock and to our conversation. My dripping-wet daughter remained full of unanswered questions.

"What are you trying to accomplish with these DRIP things, Papa? What is your goal? Do you want to have a million dollars?" she now wanted to know.

"A secure retirement, so you won't have to look after me in my old age," I replied.

"Good idea, Papa," she said sagely. Then, upon reflection, she asked, "What was the first company you bought?"

"Well, I bought several at the same time," I replied.

With a toss of her long hair, she demanded, "Well, which ones? How did you get started?"

"One of the first DRIP companies I bought was AFLAC, an American insurance company. It turned out to be one of my best investments. I joined a group called the Canadian Shareowners Association, and they bought it for me. I started with just one of their shares, and now I have almost 350!"

AFLAC has a very friendly DRIP. A detailed account of my investment with them is included at the beginning of Chapter 6, but just to whet your appetite, here are the basic facts. From 1990 to mid-2000, the AFLAC share price increased from $5.10 to $64.00 (adjusted for stock splits). Because I reinvested all my dividends, my compound annual rate of return was 29.9 percent. I invested $3,800 in small amounts over six years, and it has grown to a holding of 344 shares, worth over U.S.$22,000 ($33,000 Canadian). This increase is largely because of share-price appreciation, although stock splits and dividends have added to the total growth.

Another early investment in my DRIP portfolio was BC Gas (the full story of this DRIP can be found in Chapter 5). I selected BC Gas because of British Columbia's continuing population growth, and bought a single share in 1995. Now, just over five years later, my holding totals 200 shares, worth $5,700. Recent dividends of $61.57 have been sufficient to buy over two additional shares each quarter.

AFLAC and BC Gas are good examples of where a single share can lead you over several years. Once you get started, DRIP investing is a genuine adventure. All you need to do is to take the first step.

CHOOSING YOUR FIRST DRIP COMPANY

My strong advice on choosing your first company is to buy shares in a company you know. This could mean a company whose products you use. An example would be the Ford Motor Company if you drive one of their cars or trucks. Or it could mean Sony if you love their electronic products. It could also mean the local telephone company or electric utility. Check your pile of monthly bills for ideas. (My monthly bills include Enbridge, a natural-gas utility, and the Royal Bank of Canada, Canada's largest bank. Both offer DRIPs.) Your bank can be a solid first choice; all those service fees you resent as a customer can become much more attractive when viewed from your new vantage point as an investor.

You can find lots of ideas for places to start investing in Chapters 5 and 6 of this book, which describe many of my own successful investment experiences, and Chapter 8, which offers background information about some other companies with DRIPs that seem to me to have good potential. But in the end it's your money; you'll have to make your own decision.

Chapter 4 offers some valuable guidelines for picking likely companies, including advice to "look under your nose" at all times. This rule is especially important the first time. Pick a company close to home or connected to your life in some concrete fashion. One reason for this is that, if you truly are to succeed, one of your goals must be to learn about investing. By picking a company with some additional connection, you are more likely to become curious. Find out as much as you can about the company before you buy your first share. Afterwards, follow its fortunes closely through quarterly and annual reports, news stories, and any other information you can get.

Another reason for sticking to familiar companies it that it will diminish the "lottery syndrome" in investing. This is where foolish investors presume that some company they know almost nothing about is likely to make them rich. These "story" companies are usually just that — a story. So don't look for something exotic; look in your own backyard or garage, or on your desk.

HOW MANY COMPANIES?

There is no right answer to the question of how many companies to include in your DRIP portfolio. My recommendation is that you start with a single company, but plan on rapidly reaching a portfolio of about six companies — within the first year or sooner is a reasonable objective. There are several reasons for this.

First, as discussed in Chapter 2, you gain safety through diversification. This means owning several companies, ideally in a range of industries and geographic areas. Diversification is just a fancy word for spreading your risk, or, even more plainly, not putting all your eggs in the same basket. Think of it this way: If your sole DRIP investment is an electric utility in one city or province, a number of things could harm the value of the investment. That region could be hit, as parts of eastern Canada were, by a savage ice storm that damages utility lines. Rather than a natural disaster, an economic disaster could strike. By spreading out your investment across several companies in different sectors of the economy and different geographical locations, you will dramatically reduce the impact of any single negative event.

Another good reason to invest in several DRIPs is that it will help you learn to compare companies. Each quarter you should review the reports from each company and decide which ones are delivering the best results. You can then decide to flow more of your dollars to the best performers; you could periodically add a bonus investment in the top long-term performer. You will learn a great deal about the companies from their annual reports. The more investment information you absorb, the more generally savvy and successful an investor you'll become.

Finally, investing in six companies will translate into six monthly or quarterly opportunities to invest directly. You are more likely to send additional money, even very small amounts, to several companies. If you have only one DRIP investment, your incentive will be diminished.

For these three reasons — safety through diversification, learning through comparison, and increased incentive to invest — a portfolio of at least six companies is recommended. Of course, you can add many more as time goes by. As noted above, I have 44 DRIPs — 16 Canadian ones and a further 28 American. This is perhaps too many, particularly for the beginning investor. The paper generated by 44 annual reports and 176 quarterly reports is a bit much. I would suggest an upper limit of 20 or 25 companies in total.

YOUR COMPANY RESEARCH FILE

Once you have investments, you'll need to keep track of them. You should start a file for each company, and into that file should go all information about the company. Your monthly or quarterly account statements will become the core of that file. (As I mentioned in Chapter 1, be sure to retain all your statements to allow calculation of your cost base if you sell or are forced to sell by a merger or takeover.)

The annual reports and quarterly reports from the company should also go into its file. To prevent your house being taken over by paper, I recommend keeping only the most recent two or three quarterly reports and the last two annual reports.

Maintaining such a file is not an onerous task. Each company will require a file no bigger than a school notebook. The key is to be organized, putting each statement into the file as soon as it arrives.

Note that in most cases you need to ask for quarterly reports in order to receive them. I strongly recommend that you do so for every company in which you are a shareholder. It's free, and it's easy. Once a year you will receive a package of information from each company that contains five separate items: the annual report, a proxy ballot, a mail-back envelope, an information circular, and a registration card for receiving quarterly statements. Simply fill out and mail back the card, which indicates that you are a shareholder and that you do want to receive quarterly reports. This is an important part of your ongoing research and monitoring of the company. If you do not mail back the card, the company will stop sending the quarterly reports.

You can decide for yourself whether you want to vote. The proxy ballot will usually contain separate votes on board of directors, appointment of auditors, and any changes to share option plans. I vote, but this is not essential.

TRACKING YOUR PORTFOLIO

One of the benefits of a brokerage firm account is a monthly statement that lists your portfolio and its valuation. These statements have become more sophisticated over the years. Most brokers now record your original cost and the current value for each holding, as well as all dividends received and any other activity on your account, such as interest. This feature is now available free to any investor with Internet access. I use Yahoo! Finance, but there are many other places on the Internet with similar services (more on this in Chapter 7).

As a shareowner, you will want to keep track of the value of your shares. This information will be on your monthly or quarterly statements from the company, but you will probably want to check it more often. You will also want to read news stories about your companies and the industries they are in, adding any important ones to your file. Other useful information items to keep an eye on are analysts' reports on the companies' prospects, detailed yields, and other performance indicators.

Yahoo! and similar services make tracking this information very easy. But you do not need to be on the Internet or even own a computer to be a DRIP investor. You can track performance with a pen and notebook if you have not yet entered the computer age. Just look at each monthly or quarterly statement when it arrives; most statements list the total value of your shares. Simply compare each new statement to the one before. If the total is not calculated, it is an easy task to multiply the number of shares you hold by the current price. All company statements will provide information on the precise number of shares you own, often to three decimal places. The statement will also give you the share price as of the statement date. For an up-to-date price, your daily newspaper is the easiest source.

SETTING GOALS

The setting of goals is very personal. Your goals must reflect your own financial situation and aspirations. They must be realistic, not a mere wish or fantasy. Goals can be large and distant (e.g., to have a portfolio worth $100,000 or $1 million in 20 years) or they can be simple and immediate (e.g., to put away $50 or $100 each and every month). Goals can speak to a determined life plan, such as retirement at age 55 or 60, or they can simply relate to the ultimate size of the portfolio in dollars or shares.

Multiple goals may be the best route. You could set a monthly savings goal — a minimum amount to be invested — as a discipline. You could also set interim targets, such as 10 shares of each company, or 100 shares in total. After you have been investing for a few years, you might calculate your end point and decide to set an age-related target for your portfolio to reach: the amount you want for retirement.

My own initial goal had simplicity and modesty to commend it. I decided that a first goal would be to own 10 shares of each of the DRIP companies in which I had initially invested. This goal took the first year to attain substantially. Probably a dollar-cost strategy would have been better — a goal of $500 per company, perhaps. I chose the share number because it was easier to track.

Having reached the 10-share threshold, I set a much more ambitious goal. I would seek to increase my holdings to 100 shares of each company. With 44 companies in the two portfolios, I was making a commitment to 4,400 shares. I am still working to attain this goal by the end of 2000 (the technical end of the millennium — the world celebrated early!). This goal is more affordable in companies with a share price of $20 than those such as IBM and Mobil, where the share price exceeds $100.

In some companies my investment exceeds the 100 shares by a wide margin, often because of stock splits and stock dividends. For example, my ownership of AFLAC is 344 shares, due in large measure to two-for-one stock splits in both 1996 and 1998.

My future goal, which will occupy the first decade of the new millennium, will be to increase my DRIP portfolio to 1,000 shares of each company. Achieving this will take me to a total of 44,000 shares.

When this goal is met, likely in 2010, I will be ready to convert my savings plan to an income plan, which is part of my long-term financial goal. With the simple return of a form, each company can be directed to start forwarding my dividends to my bank account instead of reinvesting them. The beauty of this approach is that I can convert to income the dividends of one company, or several, or all of them. This way I can phase in my retirement income while preserving the tax-free growth within my RRSP for another decade, until I am compelled to begin to take it out at age 69. The

DRIP strategy provides an excellent range of options, both when you invest and when you convert your investment to income.

HELP ALONG THE WAY: INVESTORS' ASSOCIATIONS

Two extremely helpful starting organizations for DRIP investors are the Canadian Shareowners Association in Canada and the National Association of Investors Clubs in the United States. Both offer low-cost investing programs and an easy way to buy your first share in many corporations.

Canadian Shareowners Association

The Canadian Shareowners Association (CSA) and its magazine, *Canadian Shareowner*, first got me started in the DRIP investing game. At the time, *Canadian Shareowner* offered a program to assist individual investors in buying their first share in a range of companies. Once you owned your first share, you could buy directly from the company or from its transfer agent, usually a trust company. I acquired my first shares in over 30 companies through the CSA.

Membership offers access to the CSA's thinking on how to separate "Great" stocks from "Grief" stocks — valuable insight for the beginning investor. I recently renewed my own membership in the CSA and received a welcome letter from the association's president and founder, John Bart. His letter describes the CSA approach and promotes their education program, which I highly recommend.

The CSA has now put together a new approach, which it calls the LCIP, or Low Cost Investing Program. This program is open only to Canadians resident in Canada. There are fees involved: initially, a membership fee in the CSA itself, and then there are fees for opening an LCIP account and for purchasing stocks. The reinvestment of dividends is free.

I have to be candid about the LCIP. I am more comfortable dealing directly with the companies in which I am a shareholder. Mind you, I do get, as previously noted, a lot of paper. The LCIP route has more and higher fees than the direct approach, but for those who are less of a pack rat than I am, it might well be a worthwhile way to go.

The LCIP includes a broad spectrum of companies in Canada and the United States. Full details can be obtained from

Low Cost Investing Program (LCIP)
Canadian Shareowners Association
2 Carlton Street, Suite 1317
Toronto, Ontario M5B 1J3
Phone: 416-595-9600
Fax: 416-595-0400
E-mail: lcip@shareowner.ca

The list of companies appears in Chapter 7, Useful Resources for the DRIP Investor.

National Association of Investors Clubs

The National Association of Investors Clubs (NAIC) assists both individual investors and investment clubs. Since 1951 NAIC has helped over three million small investors start their own investment plans. It bills itself as "where Wall Street and Main Street meet." Among other services, which are detailed on an excellent Web site, NAIC offers its own Low Cost Investing Plan.

A membership fee in NAIC itself costs $39 a year. Then there are fees for opening an LCIP account: $7 per company and the costs of purchasing stocks. Reinvestment of dividends is free. The NAIC LCIP includes 140 companies in the United States, ranging from AT&T to Office Depot.

Your NAIC membership offers access to the organization's thinking on how to succeed as a beginning investor. You also receive their magazine, *Better Investing*. For more details on the NAIC or its LCIP, contact the association or check out its Web site, where there is a first-class set of questions and answers.

National Association of Investors Clubs
Phone: 877-275-6242
Web site: www.better-investing.org/

GO FOR IT!

You are now ready to take the first step into DRIP investing. Go ahead!

The key is to act. Unlike the first step with a broker, where you might be risking thousands of dollars, here you can start small and add as you gain knowledge and confidence. Begin with just a single company you know well and diversify quickly to six or so. Start a file for each stock. Set goals. If you need help, make use of the expertise of an investors' association. That's really all you need to do to get started. Then you need to keep going, adding a little more to your investments every month while your dividends buy still more shares for you. You will also have an incentive and reminders in the form of the monthly statements you receive.

Your DRIP portfolio will give you an outlet for your knowledge and insight as you choose where to put your new investment dollars to work each month or each quarter. Often I read a quarterly or annual report and think, "I must buy some more shares of this company, because they are doing everything right." At other times I hold back to see if a company can fix problems they have encountered.

A little nervous about your own investor savvy? Don't worry — just keep reading! Chapter 4 will give you a quick course in "investment tradecraft," arming you with some guidelines for choosing and evaluating investments as you embark on your DRIP adventure.

Chapter 4

Investment Tradecraft
Be Your Own
Investment Advisor

IN MY PREVIOUS BOOK, *MILLION-DOLLAR STRATEGY*, I SET FORTH the investment lessons I had learned in 13 years of building my own retirement fund. It took me the better part of a decade to realize and fully articulate the lessons learned from my experience as principles of a strategy. That book dealt with various kinds of investing, mostly on a larger scale, but the lessons are just as applicable to DRIP investing.

MY INVESTMENT TRADECRAFT
Stealing a term from spy novels, I summarized my thinking in seven rules of investment "tradecraft," as follows:

1. Be a contrarian. Go against the conventional wisdom.
2. Look for value where others are not looking — including under your nose.
3. Invest in individual companies, not the market.
4. Research, research, research. Read all available documents.
5. Be patient!
6. Load up on a stock when you have a strong view.
7. Make good investments steadily. Don't just wait for the great ones.

This investment tradecraft formed the basis of an investing philosophy that allowed me to build a retirement nest egg of over $1 million, and continues to serve me well today.

My view of investment tradecraft can be summarized even more succinctly in the following two principles:

1. Look under your nose.
2. Do your homework.

The first principle is not just a figure of speech; there really are investment bargains right under your nose. Each and every one of us knows some territory: the place we work, the place we live, the places we shop, the products we buy, even the monthly bills we pay. Peter Lynch, legendary manager of the Fidelity Magellan mutual fund and author of several fine books on investment, claims that many of his greatest investments were the result of trips with his kids to his local mall. Insight can come from your daily surroundings and from simple questions. If you are a teacher, is there a new classroom computer that is better? If you are a parent, what brands of clothing do your children demand? Finding opportunities is not determined by whether you are on the fiftieth floor on Bay Street or in the modesty of your main-street home. It is determined by your willingness to look and see and learn.

The second principle — do your homework — requires both learning and doing. You must have the courage to believe in your own analysis and to put your money where that analysis takes you. Research and analysis can tell you, for example, when a company's assets are far more valuable than its stock price. The necessary research is sometimes made easy by a clear, accurate annual report. In other situations, evaluating the true asset value is much more difficult. This "due diligence" — the essential research effort — is the key to doing well.

Hidden investments may offer exceptional values. Reading an annual report was the pivotal event in my first successful investment. Without that annual report I would never have known of a particular company's hidden asset value. Conversely, every existing shareholder of that company received the same report, but not all of them chose to buy additional shares.

The key to understanding any company is to start with their

own audited statements, which are included in the annual report. What are the assets of the company? What are the liabilities? Are there hidden or undervalued assets? The lesson is to get the information, conduct the research, and then trust your own analysis. The key information is the financial information. Often in corporate annual reports the surrounding verbiage has an optimistic, almost Pollyanna-like tone to it. You need to penetrate beyond the buoyant rhetoric and examine the real numbers. Answering simple questions such as "Are revenues and profits growing or shrinking?" or "Is the company earning profits for shareholders?" can provide important guidance for the investor.

Investments come in all shapes and sizes. The skills you must develop are those of analysis and judgment. And your task is ongoing — you need to continue to exercise judgment as you add to your investments over time. My own day-to-day decisions for my DRIP dollars are shaped by information I receive from each company and from the financial newspapers, television (largely CNBC), and the Internet. Every month I decide which DRIPs I should direct new dollars towards. My criteria are straightforward. I consider the earnings and other indicators of company performance. If I see promising results ahead, I buy more shares. Occasionally a merger will create lower share prices, uncertainty in the market, and a buying opportunity. (I also try to direct funds towards those companies where I am well short of my 100-share goal, but only if they offer attractive value.)

Along my investment journey there have been many mistakes (some painful) but also a number of wonderful moments. There are few pursuits more satisfying than finding a company that is doing everything right, investing in its shares, and having other investors verify your confidence by bidding up the price of the shares. Of course, sometimes it seems as if finding value in the stock market is an enterprise requiring the inquisitive spirit of Sherlock Holmes, the determination of Winston Churchill, and the patience of Job. But the payoffs — in satisfaction, excitement, learning, and, of course, profit — make it all worthwhile. For me, investing is adventure.

DRIP investing follows the same basic principles as any other investment, whether the principles are articulated by Peter Lynch or myself, in that you are primarily seeking to build value. You simply focus on a slightly smaller universe of companies — those with DRIPs.

On the next few pages, I'll offer some further thoughts on each of my seven rules, along with comments on how they relate particularly to the DRIP strategy.

RULE 1 — BE A CONTRARIAN

The first lesson is not to be afraid to go against conventional wisdom. Swimming against the current is not a good strategy for crossing a river, but it works well when investing.

The essence of being a contrarian is to go against the herd. When the herd is chasing Internet stocks, a contrarian is investing in utilities. The merit in this approach derives in largest measure from cyclical swings in fashion. Buy the dark suit, because it will come back into fashion before too long! Stocks in out-of-favour companies are often available at bargain prices, compared to the hot flavour of the month. This approach is fully applicable to a DRIP strategy. In fact, out-of-favour utility or other companies offering DRIPs may be a good value play.

Of course, simply being out of favour is not enough to recommend a stock. After all, Bre-X was out of favour after it turned out there was no gold in their Indonesian mining properties, and for very good reason. You need to marry a nonconformist, skeptical approach to research and a search for value.

Markets are driven by two basic human emotions: fear and greed. To succeed as an investor requires a healthy dose of each emotion and a contrary personality. When the mob of investors is fearful, it is time for a little bold greed. When investors become filled with greed, turn fearful. You must be able to be both patient and decisive at all times. If this sounds too much like a golf instructor who, after 20 different posture-shaping commands, suggests that you relax, it should! Investing calls for the same curious mixture of skills.

RULE 2 — LOOK WHERE OTHERS ARE NOT LOOKING

My own best early investment was one I literally walked through on a daily basis. The old Grain Exchange Building in Winnipeg was on my route from my office to the bank. While passing through the building one day, I noticed an annual report for a company named the Traders Building Association. Out of simple curiosity I picked it up, and discovered that the Grain Exchange Building was owned by this company. In addition, the company owned a portfolio of stocks and bonds. Reading the statements in the annual report, I saw that the value of this portfolio was greater than the total price of the company's shares. By my calculation, selling off the stock-and-bond portfolio would allow investors to recoup the purchase price, leaving the building as a free asset.

With all this in mind, I set out to buy shares in the Traders Building Association. This was one of my first ventures into investing, and it proved to be fairly difficult. The Winnipeg Stock Exchange opened for only a few hours of trading each week, and the shares rarely traded at all. I eventually managed to buy 300 shares at a price of $90 each. And my analysis proved to be correct. Eighteen months later a Winnipeg entrepreneur made a takeover bid for Traders Building Association. Ultimately the shares were redeemed by the successful bidder for $184.25 apiece. My original $27,000 investment sold for a grand total of $51,141 — a gain of over $24,000, or 89 percent. This experience taught me early on the importance of looking under your nose. Your daily walks can lead you to an investment too, but only if your eyes are open and looking for it.

A DRIP focus on the companies that send you monthly bills fits this principle. Think about it. Imperial Oil sends you a gasoline bill

— you invest in their DRIP. TransAlta sends you a bill for the natural gas that heats your home — you invest in their DRIP. Bell South bills you for the telephone in your teenage daughter's room — you invest in their DRIP. The Bank of Montreal sends you an overly large MasterCard bill — you buy shares in the Bank of Montreal. These companies are right under your nose.

You can get even with those annoying companies that bill you every month by buying their shares. Even though you won't ever be able to stop their bills, you can start to own a piece of their action. You can take some small measure of satisfaction that you are an owner as well as a customer.

If you are a long-time customer, you will also have some insight into company performance. You need to add to this knowledge by reading annual reports. You can also check on the Internet to see what professional analysts think of their prospects. You can build a successful DRIP portfolio without ever going beyond your monthly bills.

RULE 3 — INVEST IN COMPANIES, NOT THE MARKET

Investing in companies, not the market, has been a central theme of my investing philosophy. I have learned through experience that a company's obscurity is not a barrier to a profitable investment.

Mutual fund manager Peter Lynch has plenty of excellent advice on investing. He notes the advantage that individual investors have over professional fund managers:

> While a fund manager is more or less forced into owning a long list of stocks, an individual has the luxury of owning just a few. That means you can afford to be choosy and invest only in outfits that you understand and that have a superior product or franchise with clear opportunities for expansion. You can wait until the company repeats its successful formula in several places or markets (same-store sales on the rise, earnings on the rise) before you buy the first share.

If you put together a portfolio of five to ten of these high achievers, there's a decent chance one of them will turn out to be a 10-, a 20-, or even a 50-bagger, where you can make 10, 20, or 50 times your investment. With your stake divided among a handful of issues, all it takes is a couple of gains of this magnitude in a lifetime to produce superior returns. (Peter Lynch, in *Worth* magazine, March 1997)

One great strength of the DRIP approach is that you *can* invest only in individual companies. You avoid "buying the market" and rising and falling with it. The value of your portfolio of DRIP stocks will not be immune from movement in the market, but it will be less volatile than the broader market.

I have mentioned before that one of the great follies of beginning investors is getting trapped into a lottery view of the market. The rise and fall of the TSE 100, the Dow Jones, or the more volatile NASDAQ index is captivating, but it's a diversion. The idea is to buy individual, hopefully excellent companies. Certainly you are seeking companies that will be in business for 20 or 30 years, or perhaps longer. You are indifferent to the market's gyrations. You need to focus on the actual business of the companies in which you own shares. Once you get beyond flights of fancy about buying some undiscovered dot-com and making billions, you can get serious about investing in real companies.

What will serve you well as an investor is careful attention to individual companies. Leave the rise and fall of the market to the mob of commentators who explain, day by day, the reasons for enormous changes that are based on minor events.

RULE 4 — RESEARCH, RESEARCH, RESEARCH
Read everything you can get your hands on and make time to read. There is no such thing as too much research when it comes to investing. Your DRIP companies themselves will supply you with lots of useful reading material. Once you are the owner of a single

share you will receive the companies' own reports. Read them all, but read skeptically. You will also find lots of information about many companies on their Web sites.

I have always been a reader, and the financial world provides a never-ending stream of reports, studies, and analysis to be read. I am an avid reader of business magazines such as *Forbes*, *Fortune*, *Canadian Business*, *Inc.*, *Fast Company*, *Worth*, *Success*, and *The Economist*, among others. I tear out articles that refer to companies that pique my interest and maintain an ideas file, which always provides a good source of leads from which to draw for further research. Many of these leads turn out to be dead ends, but once in a while a true gem is uncovered this way. Sometimes I explore a company by purchasing a few initial shares to gain access to their information flow, although this is not essential. Companies will send you their annual and quarterly reports simply for the asking, and finding information on specific companies has become vastly easier and faster with the advent of the Internet. Corporate Web sites often contain not just annual reports, but current, up-to-the-minute press releases and timely quarterly and special reports.

By setting up a free account on Yahoo! as described in Chapter 7, you can instantly receive all the news about individual companies. If you don't have access to the World Wide Web at home, you can tap into a wealth of information through Internet connections at your local library or at work. There are also excellent business magazines and journals available at your local newsstand or library. If you read about a company embarking on a new and interesting venture, follow it up. Headlines like "Local Electric Utility to Sell Natural Gas" or "Telco to Lay Fibre Optic Cable" are worth checking out.

It is also necessary to research the industry within which a company operates to ensure that trends are positive. There is no point in owning shares in the best buggy-whip company, only to discover you're now in the automobile age! Many of the same sources that are helpful for company information are also places to seek industry information.

As I recommended in Chapter 3, you should start a file for each DRIP company you invest in. Your monthly or quarterly DRIP account statements should be the core of that file. The most recent annual reports and quarterly reports from the company should also go in there. (Remember that, while you probably don't need more than the last few annual and quarterly reports, you must keep *all* your DRIP statements to allow calculation of your cost base if you choose to sell or are forced to do so by a merger or takeover.) Add any relevant news clippings, photocopies of magazine articles, or printouts of information you have found on the Web. You should also start a file for any company you are considering buying, so you can gather in one place the information you'll need to make your decision. If you have several investments in the same industry, you could also start files for separate industries, such as steel or gas utilities.

Keeping these files is not an onerous task. Each company will require a file that will be no bigger than a good-sized school notebook. The key is to be organized and put each statement into the file as you receive it. If you build substantial DRIPs, you may need a small, two-drawer filing cabinet. (After six years of DRIP investing I have a stack of files about 18 inches high. Even with 44 separate DRIPs, only now am I considering buying that filing cabinet, and to date I would need only one of the two drawers.)

RULE 5 — BE PATIENT!

The most important lesson, one never fully learned by many investors (myself included), is that great patience is often required to realize a stock's full value. One of the world's most successful investors, Warren Buffett, takes the "buy-and-hold" approach. In many cases he has held the same stocks for decades. The DRIP strategy reinforces the virtue of patience. No broker is calling you to urge a switch to the hot stock of the day. You are allowed to be patient without having to fight temptation.

A DRIP strategy is for the patient. Your key goal is income in your retirement years. This is the most buy-and-hold approach of all time — the whole idea is never to sell! Of course, if some disaster befalls one of your DRIP companies, you should sell it. But as long as steady growth and solid dividends are in evidence, stick with it.

RULE 6 — LOAD UP WHEN YOU HAVE A STRONG VIEW

The next critical lesson is focus. When you are convinced of the value of a company's shares, buy as much as you can. There were periods in which Warren Buffett held as few as three securities in his multi-billion-dollar company. Although this may appear a little *too* focused, the result was excellent.

For a DRIP investor, "load up" is a relative term. But if, through your reading of annual reports and other research, you decide that one of your companies has great potential, there is nothing to prevent you from buying extra shares. Even an extra $100 or $200 now can make a difference in the long run. On the few occasions when I became truly excited about the prospects of a company in my DRIP portfolio, I gritted my teeth and wrote a cheque for a few thousand dollars instead of the usual $50 or $100.

RULE 7 — MAKE GOOD INVESTMENTS STEADILY

You can pass up a lot of good investments while waiting for the great one. Good baseball players know that a high long-term batting average is more important than trying for a home run every time. As in baseball, the key decision is to assess every pitch. Is it a ball or a strike? Is it a potential home run or a safe bunt? This principle is central to the DRIP strategy. You invest a little in each of a number of good companies. You are not waiting for the next Yahoo! or Microsoft. You are basing your investment plan on long-established, stable companies that pay dividends.

There are, of course, a few companies offering DRIPs that have demonstrated a capacity to grow and achieve extraordinary investor returns over many years. I have been fortunate to invest in AFLAC and Nortel Networks, both of which fit this category. But how do you know which company will be the one to take off this way? One clue to identifying possible high-growth companies is their track record of growth to date. Steady growth of revenue and profits in the 20-percent range is a strong positive indicator. History does repeat itself. The next problem is in knowing when that long run of growth may be slowing; watch for signs such as disappointments in quarterly earnings.

Obviously, if you can take part in a terrific success story like AFLAC, so much the better. But don't put off investing until you've found a company you think is a superstar candidate. And if you do find one, don't (as mentioned before) put all your eggs in one basket. In the long run, your best bet is a number of good, solid investments.

All of this does not mean that most DRIPs are dull, slow-growth companies. Quite the opposite! Because of the store of value in many of these companies, large gains are possible. The digital revolution is changing mature industries, such as telephone and electric utilities, into rapid-growth opportunities for investors. Because these long-established companies have real assets, they will be less vulnerable to the collapse of the Internet bubble market when that day of reckoning arrives. You will still be using your telephone and paying your gas and electric bills well into the new millennium.

A TREND-BASED INVESTMENT APPROACH

In addition to the principles articulated above, it is worth considering industry, economic, and cultural trends when choosing investments. Generally, investing needs to be rooted in fundamental movements within the economy. Some of these trends, or themes, are quite visible; others are more subtle.

Some of my own investment choices, both DRIP and non-DRIP, have been influenced by this approach. Often, successful investments result from a careful analysis of a clear trend evident in everyday life. The insight comes in following the new trend or idea through to its logical result, then identifying a company, or several companies, likely to benefit from it. A few examples from my own experience are outlined below.

Go West, Young and Old Canadians!

The evolution of North America has resulted in a steady migration to the south and west. In Canada, this means towards British Columbia. In the early 1990s, for example, the province was booming. A poll showed that a majority of Canadians would move to B.C. if they had an opportunity. In addition to migration from the rest of Canada, British Columbia was also drawing a large number of wealthy immigrants from Asia, particularly Hong Kong. With Britain poised to return Hong Kong to China, many of the colony's citizens who favoured a free-enterprise approach were looking for a new home. Vancouver's climate, large Chinese community, and affordable homes drew substantial migration from Hong Kong. My identified investment theme became the growing population of Canada's westernmost province.

What companies would benefit from this in-migration? My thought was that every new resident of British Columbia would have two certain basic requirements. They would each need a telephone, and they would also need natural gas to heat their new homes. The two companies certain to benefit from this growth would be BC Gas and BC Telecom. BC Gas is the natural-gas utility that supplies both residential and commercial markets. As the number of homes and businesses in B.C. increases, so does the demand for natural gas. BC Telecom would enjoy the same increase in business from an expanding population. In addition, new residents of B.C. would likely be phoning back home to their families. Long-distance calls to Hong Kong and Saskatchewan would certainly fuel BC Telecom profits, I concluded.

This theme caused me to invest in the DRIPs offered by these two B.C. utilities. And as the economy of neighbouring Alberta expanded, based on a boom in oil and gas prices, I reasoned that the same logic could apply to Alberta utilities. On the strength of this theme I added the Alberta phone company, Telus. I also added TransAlta Corp., an Alberta power utility, and TransCanada PipeLines, a natural-gas pipeline company. Since then, BC Tel and

Telus have merged. The two DRIPs also merged, and the resulting company is more valuable than its founding partners. The new Telus continues to allow me to benefit from economic and population growth in both Alberta and British Columbia.

The Light Bulb Goes On

For another example, consider the electric utility sector. Across North America there are perhaps 110 electric utilities. Historically, these companies' shares traded largely on the basis of their yields. (Yield is simply the dividend divided by the share price. A $1 dividend on a $10 stock means a yield of 10 percent.) Interest rates drove the level of utility stock prices in an inverse relationship: If interest rates went up, utility stocks went down.

This piece of conventional wisdom caused many investors to overlook fundamental changes in this sector. When change hits an industry, the old rules fall by the wayside. The new reality of the electric utility industry is solid growth for its product (electric power) that is being driven by economic growth and by the needs of the Internet. As well, deregulation of the sector means that prices can rise in response to demand. Mergers are racing through this once stodgy industry. A likely outcome is that the 110 utilities will consolidate down to perhaps no more than 20 much larger national or regional utilities. Investors will benefit either by being bought out at a higher price or by owning shares of a much more valuable company.

One utility that exemplifies this trend is now called Xcel. When I first invested in it, this utility was called Public Service of Colorado. Later it merged with another utility and became New Century Energies. More recently, New Century merged with Northern States Power to become Xcel. Shareholders have benefited in two fundamental ways from these mergers. First, costs have been reduced. Second, the geographic reach of the merged utility is much broader. Xcel is a more valuable company than either New Century or Public Service of Colorado was. (The full story of my experience with Public Service of Colorado and its successors is told in Chapter 6.)

The trend towards consolidation among utilities, together with the fact that many offer DRIPs and most pay decent dividends, makes them ideal candidates for inclusion in a DRIP portfolio.

Banking on Banks

Another area of significant opportunity is American banks. Unlike Canada, where a handful of national banks dominate the sector, the United States has a system that, until recently, banned national banks. The U.S., therefore, has tens of thousands of local banks. Recent legislative changes, however, have cleared the way for the United States to follow Canada into a situation where a few large national banks prevail. By enrolling in DRIPs with successful American banks, you can participate in the share-price appreciation flowing from banking consolidation. (My own picks among the U.S. banks, which include Huntington Bancshares and Wells Fargo, are described in greater detail in Chapter 6.)

CONCLUSIONS

Almost any organized and logical approach to investment fundamentals will get you off to a good start. The main idea is to focus on the value of the company in which you are placing your hard-earned dollars. You can judge this value by carefully examining a few key measures, such as earnings and earnings growth. Armed with the simple rules presented in this chapter, some attention to trends, some reading of reports, and a few dollars, you can launch your own DRIP investment portfolio now — and successfully manage it for years to come.

Chapter 5

The True North
My Favourite Canadian DRIPs

SINCE I AM A CANADIAN, THE FACT THAT A LARGE PORTION OF my investments is in Canada is important to me for patriotic reasons. As well, however, there are lots of terrific companies in Canada, many of them with DRIPs. At the time of writing, I held 2,650 shares in 16 different Canadian DRIPs.

My Canadian portfolio began in 1994, with a few DRIP investments that totalled fewer than 50 shares. By May of 1996 I had accumulated a total of 559 shares in 15 separate companies (although in four of those companies I held but a single share). The total value of the portfolio was $8,600.

By October 1996 the totals had increased to 824 shares and a value of $16,850. By then I was hooked on DRIP investing. I had come to enjoy reading the monthly and quarterly statements. Even the tiny early dividends encouraged me to make further investments. By adding an average of 37 shares per month over the next three years, I reached a total of 2,779 shares by October 2000. The total value of my DRIP portfolio then exceeded $95,000 Canadian.

DRIP investing has not only been profitable for me, it has increased my learning about Canadian companies and their business activities. The 16 companies in my Canadian portfolio represent an important cross-section of Canada's economy. They also represent some important investment trends. Banking, several utilities, a closed-end investment fund with many investments of its own, oil

My Canadian Portfolio as of October 5, 2000

Company	Business	Shares Held	Market Value
Alberta Energy	energy	57	$3,610
Aliant (Bruncor)	telecommunications	221	$8,234
BCE	telecommunications	82	$2,942
BC Gas	gas utility	198	$5,504
Canadian General Investments	diversified	413	$4,749
Canadian Pacific	energy and transport	138	$5,520
Dofasco	steel	159	$3,679
Enbridge	gas utility	109	$3,771
Fortis	electric utility	115	$3,915
Imperial Oil	integrated oil	245	$9,381
National Bank	banking	234	$5,709
Nortel Networks	digital equipment	244	$23,649
Nova Chemicals	chemicals	149	$4,127
Telus	telecommunications	145	$5,731
TransAlta	utility	156	$2,958
TransCanada PipeLines	utility	109	$1,526
Total: 16 companies		**2,779 shares**	**Can$95,074**

and gas, steel, and high technology are all part of the portfolio because I think there is growth in those sectors. All of these diverse enterprises come together in my modest DRIP portfolio. My DRIP-shaped window on the Canadian economy comes with 16 annual reports and 64 quarterly reports, as well as daily updates from my Yahoo! portfolio manager (see Chapter 7).

I am pleased with the progress of my Canadian investments. For me, Canada is my home and the true north, strong and free. I try not to worry that the Canadian stock markets badly underperformed American markets in the 1990s. In the first half of 2000 the

Toronto Stock Exchange dramatically outperformed both New York and the NASDAQ. In fact, it was up 20 percent in that period, outperforming nearly every other stock exchange in the world, while the Dow Jones Index was down nearly 10 percent. Maybe the new century will belong to Canada! In any case, as a DRIP investor, I am taking a long-term view.

WORLD LEADERS

While undertaking my research for this book, I discovered something called the Dow Jones Sustainability Group Index (DJSGI).

The DJSGI is the world's first family of global equity indexes, tracking the performance of the 200 leading sustainability-driven companies in 68 industry groups in 22 countries. The DJSGI, which was selected from the Dow Jones Global Index of nearly 3,000 companies in 33 countries, was launched in Switzerland by Dow Jones Indexes and Zurich-based researcher Sustainable Asset Management. It represents a market capitalization of U.S.$4.3 trillion.

I was delighted to learn that three of the four Canadian companies included in that index were already in my Canadian DRIP portfolio. I will consider adding the fourth, Suncor Energy. Long-term sustainability is exactly what you need to look for in a DRIP company.

The four Canadian firms — Dofasco, Enbridge, Suncor Energy, and TransAlta — have emerged as international leaders in their respective economic sectors on the new DJSGI. They are part of an elite list of 18 corporations that were identified as the most sustainable companies in their respective industries. Innovative technology, corporate governance, shareholder relations, industrial leadership, and social well-being were all included in the criteria for the list. Dofasco topped the steel category, Enbridge is the leader in pipelines, Suncor headed up the oil companies, and TransAlta leads the electric utility companies.

In announcing the member companies of its index, the DJSGI commented that

The concept of corporate sustainability has long been very attractive to investors because of its aim to increase long-term shareholder values. Sustainability-driven companies achieve their business goals by integrating economic, environmental, and social growth opportunities into their business strategies. These sustainability companies pursue these opportunities in a proactive, cost effective and responsible manner today, so they will outpace their competitors and be tomorrow's winners.

According to the index's scoring parameters, no other country has more top-ranked sustainability companies than Canada. Japan and Finland tied for second with three leading companies each, followed by the U.S., Germany, and Norway with two, and one each for the Netherlands, Finland, Switzerland, Sweden, and France. Canadian investments clearly have a great deal to offer for the long-term investor. I've been able to benefit from this fact, as my experience on the following pages demonstrates. You can, too!

OIL AND GAS PERFORMERS: NO MORE DINOSAURS TO DIE

An investor once remarked that he liked oil and gas companies because there were no more dinosaurs left to die — not a bad summary of why non-renewable fossil fuels have attraction. The reserves of oil and gas (which are really hydrocarbons) owe their existence to earlier geologic ages, although the death of dinosaurs was probably less of a factor in forming our current oil and gas deposits than the billions of much smaller, carbon-based life forms that lived in the ancient seas. Nevertheless, the key point is accurate: They ain't making any more of it.

I favour the natural-gas side of the industry for several reasons. It is continental in scope and much less affected by OPEC and Middle East politics. As well, the cleanliness of natural gas as a fuel is causing it to displace coal and nuclear reactors for generation of electric power. The price of natural gas is at a record level, and I believe it is headed higher. In a June 2000 speech, James Gray, founder and chair of Canadian Hunter, and one of the most knowledgeable executives in the gas patch, declared, "Houston, we have a problem." He went on to add, "The clouds are forming for another major energy issue — substantially higher natural gas prices." This is bad news for us as consumers, but as investors we can benefit.

I have several DRIP investments in the energy sector. Among my favourites are two larger exploration and development companies and two energy royalty trusts. Alberta Energy and Imperial Oil are the two larger companies. Imperial Oil is a fully integrated oil business, all the way down to the Esso gas stations where you fill up your car. Alberta Energy is a little more "natural gassy" than Imperial. Energy royalty trusts are a somewhat unusual but extremely attractive vehicle for investment. These trusts own oil and gas production wells and pay out all cash income as a distribution to unit holders. When prices go up, high yields (15 percent plus) are returned to investors. Some portions of these returns are taxable; the rest of the distribution is not taxed, as it represents a refund of capital. My two picks are Enerplus and Enermark, which are both on the Toronto Stock Exchange. Let me comment on each of these four terrific DRIPs in turn.

Alberta Energy Co.

The Alberta Energy Company (AEC) was originally incorporated in 1973 as the Alberta government's natural resource company. It owned conventional oil and natural gas reserves, bitumen-based Syncrude, and timber, coal, and fertilizer businesses. The company went public in 1975 when the Government of Alberta sold 50 percent of AEC's shares to the Canadian public. The company sold its coal, fertilizers, and timber in the early 1990s. The Government of Alberta sold its remaining 36-percent stake in AEC in 1993. Trading of AEC shares began on the New York Stock Exchange in 1995 under the AOG ticker abbreviation. Approximately 25 percent of AEC's issued common shares are now owned in the U.S.

Through 20 principal operating subsidiaries, AEC ranks as one of Canada's largest upstream (production) companies. It also has interest in midstream operations (gathering, pipeline, processing, and storage facilities), which provide reliable cash flow and add value to its upstream business. The company has grown through the years in an organic and acquisitive manner, and now ranks as sixth largest among independent natural-gas producers in North America. In Canada, AEC stands as the second largest producer of natural gas and sixth largest of oil. AEC's operating units function in a semi-autonomous manner through a very flat organizational structure.

AEC has a high ratio of reserves to actual production. This means its risk of having to reinvest in new drilling on short notice is low, which helps protect cash flow — and that ultimately facilitates long-term production growth. Also note that AEC follows the basic tenets of a successful exploration and production company, by operating most of its own properties. Its production is concentrated geographically, and it also owns the pipelines and plants to extract the oil and gas. AEC also has an excellent base for future development in its very large holdings of undeveloped land. In oil-patch parlance, Alberta Energy is "up to its ass in gas."

Two great reasons for liking Alberta Energy are its terrific land position and its heavy focus on natural gas. Oil prices, as I mentioned above, can be volatile because they are based on factors in other parts of the world, while natural-gas prices tend to reflect conditions in North America. For many years Canadian natural gas has been "trapped" in Canada by the lack of pipeline capacity to transport it to southern markets. As of November 2000, however, that problem has been solved by the construction of the new Alliance pipeline. For this reason and because of future expected shortages of supply, Canadian gas producers will be receiving higher prices.

AEC has a fairly stable upper management. Gwyn Morgan serves as president and chief executive officer, and has been in this capacity since 1994. The chief financial officer for the last 12 years has been John Watson. AEC employs 850 people in Canada (550 office staff, 300 in the field, and 20 geotechnical specialists) and 225 abroad, primarily in Ecuador.

With a current market capitalization exceeding Can$4 billion, Alberta Energy is an industry leader. Its 4.2 trillion cubic feet of natural-gas reserves are the largest reserve of any Canadian publicly traded producer. As well, with over 900 million cubic feet per day of natural-gas sales, Alberta Energy is aiming to become the largest Canadian publicly traded producer. The company also owns 7.1 million net acres of exploration land in North America and 1.8 million net acres outside North America.

Midstream assets represent approximately 20 percent of AEC's asset base. Alberta Energy has the largest independently owned natural-gas storage facility in North America, and also owns 70 percent of AEC Pipelines LP, the largest intra-Alberta oil transporter.

Alberta Energy's Dividend Reinvestment Plan is administered by the CIBC Mellon Trust Company. My holdings of Alberta Energy amount to 57 shares, with a value of $3,610. I intend to add to this position, as I believe AEC is an excellent and profitable way to participate safely in the growing demand for natural gas in North America. Its dividends are low, but it is an energy company well positioned for the long haul.

ALBERTA ENERGY (AEC–TSE) www.aec.ca

Dividend Yield: 0.66%

Features of DRIP: A no-fee DRIP with a minimum cash option of $50 and a maximum of $5,000 per quarter.

How to Contact: CIBC Mellon Trust Company

600 Dome Tower

333 – 7th Avenue S.W.

Calgary, Alberta T2P 2Z1

Phone: 1-800-387-0825

E-mail: inquiries@cibcmellon.ca

Web site: www.cibcmellon.ca

Imperial Oil

Imperial Oil, of which 70 percent is owned by Exxon Mobil, is Canada's largest oil company, holding about 20 percent of the country's proven reserves. Exxon's merger with Mobil (for more on this, see the discussion of my Exxon and Mobil DRIPs in Chapter 6) is likely to increase Imperial's total operations in Canada. It is already one of Canada's largest natural-gas producers, and the number one refiner and marketer of petroleum products, as well as a major supplier of petrochemicals. Imperial sells more than 700 petroleum products, including gasoline, heating oil, and diesel fuel, under *Esso* and other brand names. Most of the company's production comes from fields in Alberta and the Northwest Territories. It is conducting experimental operations at Cold Lake, Alberta, using steam to recover very heavy crude from oil-sands deposits.

My initial investment in Imperial Oil was small, but in 1998 I made a major investment of $5,000. This was at a time when I believed Imperial shares to be well below their true value. The investment appears to have been timely, as oil and natural-gas prices have climbed. So, too, has the value of my Imperial Oil DRIP. Imperial Oil has bought back millions of its own shares with excess cash flow. This is a great benefit, as it increases the value of the remaining shares. I consider Imperial a safe way to participate in the Canadian oil-and-gas sector; I now own 245 shares, worth $9,381.

IMPERIAL OIL (IMO–TSE) www.imperialoil.ca

Dividend Yield: 2.07%

Features of DRIP: One share required to enrol; after that, a minimum purchase of $50.

How to Contact: Montreal Trust Company of Canada

Phone: 1-800-332-0095

TRUSTING IN OIL AND GAS

As mentioned previously, energy trusts are an investment vehicle that allows participation in oil and gas production. Their benefits include exposure to higher prices.

Enermark Income Fund

Enermark was created by the reorganization of Mark Resources in April 1996. It is an investment trust that owns oil and gas properties, but distributes its income to unit holders rather than exploring for additional oil and gas. Through acquisitions, Enermark has grown to revenues of $170 million. It has more than replaced its reserves of oil and gas each year through acquisitions. With a current dividend yield of over 15 percent, it is an excellent way to invest in oil and, even more so, in gas. Enermark offers a DRIP that features as an added bonus a 5-percent discount on shares bought with dividends. In view of the prospects for rising gas prices, its high yield, and its replacement of reserves, Enermark should be a solid DRIP investment.

ENERMARK (EIF.UW–TSE) www.enerplus.com

Dividend Yield: 18.9%
Features of DRIP: No fees; no minimum. Discount of 5% on dividend reinvestment.
How to Contact: Phone: 1-800-319-6462

Enerplus Resources Fund

Like Enermark, Enerplus is an investment trust that holds oil and gas properties. It has increased its total reserves largely through acquisitions. Also like Enermark, it has a high yield (16.5 percent), and it too offers a 5-percent discount on dividends reinvested. This is an excellent feature for the patient investor.

ENERPLUS (ERF.UN–TSE) www.enerplus.com

Dividend Yield: 19.6%
Features of DRIP: No fees; no minimum. Discount of 5% on dividend reinvestment.
How to Contact: Phone: 1-800-319-6462

I have added steadily to my total units of both Enermark and Enerplus over the years, through periods of both low and high prices for oil and gas. Over time, my cost of acquiring the units has averaged to a reasonable level. Both these trusts would be excellent DRIP investments. My own energy trust units are held in my RRSP account to simplify my tax accounting. An RRSP account, as noted previously, offers a dividend reinvestment feature, but you cannot directly purchase additional shares in this situation.

GAS PIPELINES: GETTING READY FOR THE AGE OF NATURAL GAS

Our energy use is shifting rather rapidly from coal and nuclear power to a much greater dependence on natural gas. There are two main reasons: cost and concern for the environment. Natural gas is less polluting than other fuels, and power plants are closing or being converted to natural-gas facilities. I discussed above how the emerging natural-gas economy offers investors opportunities in the production of natural gas. A second area of opportunity is in the pipelines needed to transport the gas to our homes, offices, and factories. I own four DRIPs based on this investment trend: BC Gas, Enbridge, TransAlta, and TransCanada PipeLines.

BC Gas Inc.

One of the few certainties about the future of Canada is continuing population growth in British Columbia. This migration includes an ever-increasing band of retirees moving west from the cold winters of Saskatchewan and Manitoba. Immigration from Asia has also expanded the B.C. population; in times of economic trouble in Asia, Vancouver is a safe haven. As the natural-gas utility for this western province, BC Gas will see its business grow. Each new house, apartment, or condo built in British Columbia is a new customer for BC Gas.

As well, permission has been granted for BC Gas to build a gas pipeline from the mainland to Vancouver Island, and construction is underway. This pipeline should prove a very valuable long-term asset for the utility.

The benefits of BC Gas as a DRIP investment are its long-term consistent growth and a steady dividend stream with which to buy further equity. A statement from my BC Gas account is reproduced here.

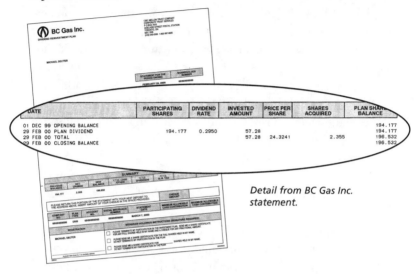

Detail from BC Gas Inc. statement.

The statement reproduced here shows a share balance of 196.532 shares, a dividend of 29.5 cents per share, and a dividend reinvestment of $57.28, buying 2.355 new shares. My holdings of BC Gas were among my earliest DRIP investments. In May 1996 I had 153 shares, worth $500; by August 2000 I had 200 shares, valued at $5,565. Most of the growth was through share-price appreciation and dividend reinvestment.

BC GAS INC. (BCG–TSE) www.bcgas.com

Dividend Yield: 4.16%

Features of DRIP: A good no-fee plan, with no cash minimum and a maximum of $20,000 per year.

How to Contact: Phone: 1-800-387-0825

Enbridge Inc.

Enbridge Inc., formerly known as IPL Energy Inc., is a leader in energy transportation, distribution, and services. As a transporter of energy, Enbridge operates, in both Canada and the United States, the world's longest pipeline system for crude oil and liquids. The company is also active in international energy projects and increasingly involved in transmission of natural gas. As a distributor of energy, Enbridge owns and operates Canada's largest natural-gas distribution company, which provides gas to 1.4 million customers in Ontario, Quebec, and New York State, and is also involved in the generation and distribution of electricity. In addition, Enbridge provides retail energy products (such as furnaces and air conditioners) and services (such as home insulation) to a growing number of Canadian and U.S. markets. The company employs more than 5,000 people, primarily in Canada, the United States, and South America.

Enbridge common shares trade on the Toronto and Montreal stock exchanges in Canada under the symbol ENB and on the NASDAQ National Market in the United States under the symbol ENBRF. In 1998 Enbridge shares outperformed the Toronto Stock Exchange 300 and their peer group. The share price increased by 8 percent, to $70.50, and annual dividends rose by 6 percent, to $2.24 per common share. The combination of share-price appreciation and increased dividends meant that, for the year ending December 31, 1998, the total return from an investment made at the beginning of 1998 was 11.7 percent. This compares well with a loss of 5 percent on a composite investment in Canadian companies whose business activities and risk levels are most comparable to Enbridge's, and with a 1.6 percent loss by the Toronto Stock Exchange 300 Composite Index.

In May 1999 Enbridge split its shares two for one. Since then shares have increased in value from just over $30 per share (post split) to just under $40 per share in October 2000. This is a further gain of 30 percent plus dividends.

Enbridge has big plans for the future, which it groups under six strategies:

1. developing core pipeline and gas distribution businesses,
2. enhancing profitability through continued application of incentive-rate mechanisms and cost-efficient operations,
3. developing natural-gas pipelines,
4. expanding internationally,
5. establishing an electric power distribution and related co-generation business, and
6. making a measured entry into unregulated retail energy services markets.

Enbridge should also benefit directly from the growth of the natural-gas economy, as discussed earlier. As a holder of 109 shares, worth $3,771, I hope these strategies and opportunities continue to increase Enbridge's earnings and its share value.

ENBRIDGE INC. (ENB–TSE) www.enbridge.com

Dividend Yield: 3.66%
Features of DRIP: No fees and no minimum cash investment; maximum quarterly investment is Can$5,000.
How to Contact: CIBC Mellon Trust Company
Corporate Trust Services
P.O. Box 7010
Adelaide Street Postal Station
Toronto, Ontario M5C 2W9
Phone: 1-800-387-0825
Web site: www.cibcmellon.ca

TransCanada PipeLines Ltd.

TransCanada PipeLines is one of the largest energy-services companies in North America. From its base in Calgary the company operates a large gas-transmission system, with 42,000 kilometres of pipeline that gathers natural gas from wells in western Canada (primarily Alberta) and delivers it to customers in eastern Canada and the United States. Its system moves 80 percent of Canada's natural-gas production and serves markets that account for 45 percent of North American gas consumption. Other activities include power generation and marketing, as well as the extraction and production of liquids from natural gas. About half the company's transmission earnings are from the Canadian Mainline, the long-distance pipeline from Alberta to the east.

With downward pressures on the regulated side of TransCanada's business, the outlook for profit growth is only modest. But this stock is very suitable for DRIP portfolios; over the long haul, it is an excellent utility company.

A 1998 merger between NOVA and TransCanada led to the spinoff of NOVA's chemical businesses into a separate company (which is also a great DRIP; see pages 82–83). The remaining pipeline and energy company is focused on its core business. Competition in energy transmission is increasing because of new pipeline construction, but TransCanada is expected to continue to be a low-cost provider. TransCanada's energy-processing business uses natural gas to produce energy and specialty chemical products that the company markets throughout the world. This part of its business has also been squeezed by lower product prices and higher natural-gas prices, which have reduced its margins and earnings. The outlook for these operations is positive, however, because of the growth of natural-gas production and the expectation of improved product prices. The U.S. demand for Canadian natural gas will sustain the business and, in my view, lead to profitable medium-term growth.

Before the merger with NOVA, TransCanada had raised its dividend every six years at an average annual rate of 8 percent. After the merger, the company reduced its dividend, causing the share price to plunge. Now, after the sell-off of all but its core assets, TransCanada is on the mend. The current dividend yield is an attractive 5.82 percent. There are, however, some risks ahead for the company:

- Rising interest rates can have a negative impact on stocks, such as TransCanada, that pay high dividends.
- The bulk of TransCanada's operations are regulated, and regulatory changes can affect the company's earnings.
- Additional pipeline capacity is being built, meaning more competition for TransCanada and possibly a negative impact on earnings.

My holdings of TransCanada are modest, consisting of 109 shares acquired as a result of the NOVA merger, and worth only $1,526. I intend to buy more soon, however, since the dividend yield is attractive and the company's pipeline capacity will be needed to meet U.S. demands.

TRANSCANADA PIPELINES LTD. (TRP–TSE) www.transcanada.com

Dividend Yield: 5.82%

Features of DRIP: Allows dividend reinvestment at 5-percent discount to market price (one of the few discounts available in major utilities). Additional cash contributions permitted quarterly, with a minimum of $50 and maximum of $10,000.

How to Contact: Montreal Trust Company of Canada
Phone: 1-800-267-6555

TransAlta Corp.

This excellent utility has two businesses: the original, regulated electric utility in Alberta and an unregulated energy company with international interests. Regulators appointed by governments determine how much money utilities can earn on their regulated businesses. These returns can be reduced by arbitrary decisions. TransAlta's regulated business has been hurt by a lower allowed rate of return — a phenomenon that will become more common in deflationary times. The unregulated business is doing very well. As noted at the beginning of the chapter, TransAlta Corp. was chosen as one of a handful of Canadian companies for the Dow

Jones Sustainability Group Index. TransAlta is less "gassy" than the three previous utilities, but will still in my view benefit from conversion to a gas-based energy economy.

TransAlta has assets and operations in Canada, New Zealand, Australia, and the United States. Its operations include electricity generation and distribution, energy services, and energy marketing. The corporation's history can be traced back to 1911. Since then it has provided electricity that is among the lowest costing and most reliable in North America. TransAlta's growth strategy is aimed at providing new and existing customers with innovative energy solutions in increasingly deregulated markets.

TransAlta has 2,455 employees and $5 billion in assets. It is the largest independent power producer in Canada and currently has six plants, either under construction or in development, in both Canada and Australia. TransAlta is Western Australia's second largest supplier of power, with five independent power projects.

My holdings of TransAlta total 156 shares, worth $2,958.

TransAlta Corp. (TA–TSE) www.transalta.com

Dividend Yield: 5.21%
Features of DRIP: A solid no-fee plan with a one-share minimum, no cash minimum, and a maximum of $5,000 per quarter.
How to Contact: CIBC Mellon Trust Company
Phone: 1-800-387-0825
Web site: www.cibcmellon.ca

OLD MA BELL BECOMES THE DIVINE MS. B

Remember when telephone companies were really boring, both as investments and as companies? Slow-growing and heavily regulated, they once offered to investors security, dividends, and little else. In the past few years, telcos, as they are now called, have become dynamic powerhouses of the digital economy and of the stock markets. In Canada there are three telcos that have a solid place in my DRIP portfolio: the venerable BCE, Aliant, and Telus.

These three companies cover most of Canada's geographic area —
and a wide range of new-economy businesses.

Convergence is the new media business theory; the idea is to
own both content and channels. Thus BCE now owns television
stations (CTV), newspapers (the *Globe and Mail*), and Internet
businesses. Time will tell whether this trend is a boon for investors.
Aliant, which is made up of formerly separate telcos in Atlantic
Canada, is no slouch in the new-economy department either,
having investments in a range of digital firms. Telus, the merged
Alberta and B.C. telephone systems, has gone national. From an
investor point of view, these companies offer higher risk than in the
good old days, but also the potential of higher returns.

BCE Inc.

Bell Canada Enterprises is Canada's largest company, with revenues
of $27.5 billion in 1998 and many employees. Key subsidiaries
include the following:

- Bell Canada
- Bell Mobility
- Bell Canada International
- Bell ActiMedia
- CTV Network
- the *Globe and Mail*

Bell Canada's local and long-distance service area includes
about 70 percent of the country's population. Its BCE Mobile
Communications subsidiary offers mobile telephone service
throughout the country. Other subsidiaries include Tele-Direct,
which publishes a variety of directories including the Yellow Pages,
and Bell Canada International, which provides telecommunications development and consulting services throughout the world.

In the spring of 1999, BCE sold 20 percent of its major subsidiary,
Bell Canada, to Ameritech for $5.1 billion in cash. This is an extremely
positive development for BCE, putting the company in a position
to offer full telecommunications capability to its customer base.

I own 82 shares of BCE now, worth $2,942. (This is after the 2000 spinoff of Nortel, which increased my total holdings of Nortel, but diminished the share value of BCE.)

BELL CANADA ENTERPRISES INC. (BCE–TSE) www.bce.ca

Dividend Yield: 3.24%

Features of DRIP: A good no-fee plan, with no cash minimum and a maximum of $20,000 per year.

How to Contact: Phone: 1-800-561-0934

Nortel Networks Corp.

In 2000 BCE spun off Nortel Networks, the crown jewel of Canadian companies. As measured by stock-market value, Nortel is Canada's most valuable company. Nortel Networks designs, develops, manufactures, markets, sells, finances, installs, and services fully digital telecommunications systems.

The company's strong and large product line gives every reason to expect it will continue to produce better than industry results. My quarterly report of March 1999, for example, shows that its revenues increased significantly, benefiting from increased sales in the wireless and broadband areas. However, its earnings suffered a net loss that quarter, largely because of the cost of the many companies Nortel is buying.

Nortel remains a first-rate technology company. It has

- a strong leadership position in optical networking, a key element of next-generation networks (NGNs);
- a good position as a provider of IP-based products, the other key element of NGNs;
- strong global carrier relationships and a reputation for carrier class reliability;
- one of the most complete communications equipment product lines in the business;
- an attractive relative valuation when compared with its major competitors, Lucent and Cisco; and

- good order flow, including another win with AT&T for wireless infrastructure, and more business from US West.

Nortel recently announced its acquisition of Periphonics, a company whose technology will apply in Nortel's push into interactive Web- and voice-based e-commerce solutions. This may not be the "sexiest" acquisition, but it is a growth area, and the numbers seem to suggest it is properly valued and should help Nortel bring its integrated voice and data solutions to market faster. For the year ending May 1999, Periphonics had revenue of $142 million, up 21 percent, and earnings of $9 million, up 100 percent. Its gross margins are about 51 percent. These numbers are all in line with or above the Nortel corporate averages.

NORTEL NETWORKS CORP. (NTL–TSE) www.nortel.com

Dividend Yield: 0.11% (However, the dividend yield is not the reason to buy.)
Features of DRIP: Allows quarterly additional cash investments of a minimum of U.S.$50 and a maximum of U.S.$5,000. (Nortel runs its business in U.S. dollars.)
How to Contact: Phone: 1-800-561-0934

Aliant Inc.

The second quarter of 1999 marked a new beginning for telecommunications and IT companies in Atlantic Canada. At annual general and special meetings across the Atlantic region, shareholders voted overwhelmingly to merge Bruncor Inc., Island Telecom Inc., Maritime Telegraph and Telephone Company Ltd., and NewTelk Enterprises Ltd. The merged entity, Aliant, began operations on June 1, 1999. The new company is filled with promise and has had some early success.

In my view, the key hidden value in Aliant lies in its information technology investments in smaller companies. These include MITI Information Technology Inc., xwave solutions inc., Island Tel

Advanced Solutions, and NBTel's IT division. Together, Aliant's information technology businesses provide a full range of IT consulting, managed network services, systems integration, and IT outsourcing services. The IT division grew further recently with xwave solutions' acquisition of Software Kinetics Ltd. This acquisition has allowed the company to extend its reach into the Ontario market as it continues to establish itself as a truly national organization.

Aliant's 1999 annual report revealed the result of this expansion in the IT division: tremendous revenue growth of 95.9 percent over the 1998 figure. In late June 1999 MITI was named to *Profit* magazine's top 100 fastest-growing businesses. Other areas of Aliant's operations are also booming. Its mobile satellite communications business is conducted through its 65 percent ownership of Stratos Global Corporation (SGB–TSE). Stratos Global reported second-quarter revenue in 1999 of $36.8 million, more than double the figure for the same period in 1998.

Through its wholly owned subsidiary Nova-Net Communications, Stratos Global is a major North American provider of VSAT (Very Small Aperture Terminals) satellite data networks. Nova-Net was recently awarded contracts worth over $1 million for the supply of satellite terminals and monitoring services for the gas pipeline running from Nova Scotia to Boston.

Aliant also has an emerging business division, which focuses on developing and nurturing new technology-based products and services for sale in Atlantic Canada and around the world. The companies in this division represent a very diverse range of businesses, including AMI Offshore (a St. John's distributor of telecom and industrial equipment), iMagicTV (which provides interactive TV services), and minority interests in InfoInterActive (a leading provider of Internet-based call-management solutions), Salter Street Films, and Salter Street New Media. Aliant feels that iMagicTV represents their largest new growth opportunity.

Today, instead of investing in a sleepy telephone utility limited by the size of its market, investors in Aliant are buying world-class innovation. The emerging Aliant businesses have access to global markets and vast growth potential.

My Aliant holdings of 221 shares were worth $8,234 in June 2000. This is a solid increase from the $4,400 value of my Bruncor holdings in 1998, prior to the merger. I have done well to date and hope for continued growth in value in the future.

ALIANT INC. (AIT–TSE) www.aliant.ca

Dividend Yield: 2.81%
Features of DRIP: A no-fee DRIP with no minimum on its cash option and a $10,000 maximum per quarter.
How to Contact: Phone: 1-800-565-2188

Telus

When I decided to invest in telephone companies in western Canada, my original goal was to enjoy the growth in population and in telephone calls. As an investor I have been surprised at the pace of consolidation in the industry. My original investments were in BC Telecom, which covered the province of British Columbia, and in Telus, which provided telephone services to residents of Alberta.

My logic rested on the rapid growth of population in those two provinces. Alberta's economy, driven by oil and gas riches and resultant low taxes, has transformed Calgary and Edmonton into Canada's fourth and fifth largest cities. Calgary is beginning to pull head offices from both Montreal (such as Canadian Pacific) and Vancouver. As discussed earlier, British Columbia, despite difficulties in its economy, has enjoyed steady population growth, primarily through immigration from colder Canadian locations and from Hong Kong. All of these new British Columbians, like ET, will need to call home.

The event I had not anticipated, when I began to build my investment through BC Telecom and Telus DRIPs, was a rapid series of industry mergers. Bigger appears to be better in the telco world. BC Telecom and Telus merged and became BCT-Telus

Communications Inc. Fortunately, they also merged their DRIP plans. As a result of this merger and dividends paid by the combined company in 1999 and 2000, my holdings had increased by October 2000 to 145 shares, worth $5,731. It also catapulted me past my 100-share goal. Next stop, by the time I retire: 1,000 shares!

TELUS (T–TSE) www.telus.com

Dividend Yield: 3.58%
Features of DRIP: Minimum of $100; maximum of $20,000. Discount of 5% on dividends.
How to Contact: Phone: 403-498-7311

IN GOOD COMPANY

My investments in the companies discussed above were sparked by economic or sectoral trends. But I've also chosen some DRIPs that are simply very good companies. Most of these are worth considering for your own DRIPs. Their business activities span the spectrum from banking to chemicals to steel to investments, yet each has a solid value proposition. Each is described in some detail below.

Assets at a Discount: Canadian General Investments Ltd.

Canadian General Investments (CGI) represents a unique situation and an unusual investment. Established in 1930, CGI is a closed-end, Canadian equities fund. It invests in Canadian companies with a view to long-term growth. CGI has a strong recent history of paying large dividends in both cash and stock. Part of the reason for these large payouts is to narrow the gap between the share price and the underlying value.

My first investment in CGI units was $47 in June 1996. This sum purchased 3.98 shares for my account at a price of $11.80 each. Later in 1996 I invested a further $200; the share price had risen to $12.80 by then. I also received 2 shares as a stock dividend in 1996. In 1997 I added 133 shares through further investment; as well, I received 3 shares through cash dividend reinvestment and 13 shares through stock dividends. In 1998 I bought a further 30 shares and received 18 shares through cash dividend reinvestment and 4 shares through stock dividends.

In 1999 I received several more shares through cash dividend reinvestment. In early 2000 I decided that CGI was significantly undervalued, and invested a further $2,000. By the end of September 2000, I had total holdings of 413 shares, worth $4,749.

One unusual feature of CGI is that, as with many closed-end trusts, it trades at a discount to its net asset value. Translated into English, this means that in September 1999 you could buy CGI shares with an underlying worth of $15.20 for only $11.10 — a 27-percent discount. That means that the total value of all the stocks CGI owns is greater than the price of its own shares. The level of the discount varies; you can check it in the financial pages of the weekly *Barron's* or on Saturdays in the *National Post*. Unlike a mutual fund, where you pay full value for your holdings and annual fees of 1 to 2.5 percent, purchasing the CGI closed-end fund gives you a discount to the real asset value. This discount, combined with their long track record of successful investments, is why CGI is a core DRIP holding for me.

To give you the flavour of CGI, their top 10 holdings as of the end of 1999 are listed on pages 74–75 with CGI's evaluations.

CGI PORTFOLIO — 10 LARGEST INVESTMENTS
AS OF DECEMBER 31, 1999

COMPANY	COST ($000S)	MARKET VALUE ($000S)	% OF TOTAL INVESTMENT PORTFOLIO
BCE Inc.	9,323	24,918	6.9

BCE has the makings of a telecommunications company of global strength. It has core investments in unusually powerful and successful Canadian and international companies. BCE's next stage of explosive growth moves closer with the unlocking of value by distribution to shareholders of all but 2% of its 39% holding in communications equipment giant Nortel Networks Corporation.

Nortel Networks Corporation	12,669	23,336	6.5

Nortel is a leading supplier of data and telephone network solutions and services into the Internet revolution that is changing the way the world communicates. A well entrenched premier infrastructure supplier, Nortel is a major beneficiary of phenomenal demand.

JDS Uniphase Canada Ltd.	7,453	18,720	5.2

Newcomer JDS Uniphase was created in 1999 through the $6.2 billion merger of JDS Fitel Inc. (Canadian) and Uniphase Corp. (American). The transaction set up JDS as the leading player in the optical networking components and modules market. Optical networking is the "solution of choice" for accommodating the bandwidth demands of surging data traffic worldwide. Customers include the major systems vendors, such as Nortel, Lucent, Cisco, and Alcatel.

CT Financial Services Inc.	6,082	11,655	3.2

CT Financial, the financial holding company for the Canada Trust group of companies, has been recognized for the coveted financial asset it is and has been acquired by Toronto Dominion Bank. It was the last of the non-bank owned major trust companies. As a result, CGI will receive significant gains from disposal for the second time since 1983. This will free approximately $12 million for reinvestment.

BCE Emergis Inc.	3,036	10,850	3.0

BCE Emergis delivers the "e-commerce building blocks" that enable its customers to conduct business electronically. It is the largest e-commerce company in Canada. Revenue potential for BCE Emergis is huge as Internet commerce grows rapidly. BCE Inc. owns 68% of BCE Emergis and provides credibility, financial backing, and relationship opportunities.

Company	Cost ($000s)	Market Value ($000s)	% of Total Investment Portfolio
Celestica Inc.	6,273	10,019	2.8

Celestica is a leading provider of electronics manufacturing services (EMS) to original equipment manufacturers (OEM) — the third largest worldwide. EMS is growing rapidly. Celestica primarily serves world-class clients in computer and communications sectors and is aggressively acquiring additional capabilities as OEMs continue to increase their outsourcing of manufacturing.

Toronto Dominion Bank	6,895	9,300	2.6

Toronto Dominion Bank is CGI's largest bank holding. It is fifth largest in Canada in assets but the largest in market capitalization and top in share performance. TD owns 89% of TD Waterhouse, the second largest discount broker in North America. The bank will expand significantly in 2000 with the purchase of CT Financial, the largest and last to be merged of Canada's great trust companies.

PMC-Sierra Inc.	5,785	9,255	2.5

Headquartered in Burnaby, B.C., NASDAQ-listed PMC-Sierra designs, develops, markets, and supports semiconductor networking solutions. The products are used globally in high-speed transmission and networking systems focused on high growth communications market segments. PMC-Sierra will benefit from the non-stop upgrades required to handle a tidal wave of digital traffic.

Falconbridge Ltd.	6,017	7,474	2.1

Falconbridge explores for, develops, processes, and markets a number of metals and minerals. The company is over 47% owned by Noranda Inc., Canada's biggest mining group and one of the world's most important nickel and cobalt producers. CGI had a 7.1% weighting in metals and minerals at year-end.

Bombardier Inc.	2,549	7,412	2.0

Bombardier is a world-wide manufacturer of aerospace, transportation, and motorized recreational products. Close to 90% of all Bombardier sales are in U.S. dollars. While the recreational division has been mildly disappointing, aerospace has been more than exceptional and rail transit contracts are a constant source of major revenues. Bombardier has been one of the most reliable long-term performers in the CGI portfolio.

Total	**66,082**	**132,939**	**36.8**

At the present time, CGI is tending toward bigger individual holdings in a continuing effort to narrow the gap between the fund's performance and the benchmark index, which compares the fund to the overall market.

CGI has a terrific long-term track record. It also offers an excellent DRIP. The table below shows that $10,000 invested in 1983 would have grown to $69,000 by 1998. Of course, a smaller investment would have experienced the same percentage gains — perfect for a DRIP investor! The cumulative value of reinvested dividends alone would be over $30,000 in 15 years. And given the modest share

Calendar Year Ending December 31	Market Value of Original Shares	Cumulative Market Value of Dividends Reinvested	Total Market Value	Total Net Asset Value
1983	$10,000	$0	$10,000	$15,144
1984	10,809	493	11,302	16,330
1985	13,824	1,200	15,024	20,215
1986	15,735	1,957	17,692	21,998
1987	11,176	1,890	13,066	20,852
1988	11,471	2,630	14,101	22,720
1989	13,529	3,865	17,394	26,073
1990	11,471	4,060	15,531	24,782
1991	12,647	5,309	17,953	28,599
1992	16,176	7,671	23,847	28,912
1993	20,294	10,607	30,901	38,012
1994	16,618	11,992	28,610	39,578
1995	17,868	14,713	32,581	46,594
1996	25,235	25,846	51,081	60,047
1997	27,618	39,241	66,859	67,917
1998	22,941	38,312	61,253	69,405
1999	20,408	34,444	4,852	72,361

Returns on a 15-Year Investment of $10,000 in CGI

price of $12 to $13, you can build a sizable share portfolio. Note that the discount mentioned above means that you start out basically ahead: Your $10,000 in 1983 would have bought over $15,000 worth of total assets.

The key point about CGI is that you can even buy a well-managed fund with the DRIP strategy — leading companies at a large discount to their true value!

CANADIAN GENERAL INVESTMENTS LTD. (CGI–TSE)
www.mma-investmgr.com

Dividend Yield: 2.11%
Features of DRIP: A $100 minimum for cash investments and a maximum of $5,000 per quarter.
How to Contact: Phone: 416-981-9633
E-mail: cgifund@mma-investingr.com

A Historical Giant: Canadian Pacific Ltd.

At one time to many investors worldwide, Canadian Pacific was Canada. In one company you got a railroad, hotels, an oil company, and global shipping. As Canada's economy has grown there is no longer one company that could be thought of as Canada, but Canadian Pacific can still do a passable imitation. It is a multidivisional company operating in the fields of transportation (Canadian Pacific Railway; CP Ships), energy and mining (87 percent of PanCanadian Petroleum; Fording Coal), and accommodation (CP Hotels).

Through the late 1980s and early 1990s, the company divested itself of about 40 percent (as measured by book value) of its holdings, choosing to retain the current five operating companies as core holdings. The incentives for this move were twofold: to reduce the large discount to underlying net asset value at which the shares of CP were trading (due in part to its large number of holdings, particularly those in which CP held less than 100-percent ownership), and to reduce the cyclical nature of its earnings by eliminating those assets in which CP had no inherent market advantage and which were, therefore, more susceptible to market forces.

Internal cash flows and proceeds from these sales have been used to strengthen the company by reinvesting in and reinforcing the competitive position of its core holdings (where it enjoys unique assets or industry franchises) and by initiating a regular and substantial share-repurchase program and a sustainable dividend.

Overall, CP is a great Canadian company. My holdings of 138 shares were worth $5,520 at the time of writing.

CANADIAN PACIFIC LTD. (CP–TSE) www.cp.ca

Dividend Yield: 1.43%
Features of DRIP: No fees for dividend reinvestment or optional cash investments. No minimum amount and a $30,000 maximum per year.
How to Contact: The Trust Company of the Bank of Montreal
129 Saint-Jacques Street, Level P, North
Montreal, Quebec H4Y 1L6
Phone: 1-800-332-0095

The Strength of Steel: Dofasco Inc.

Dofasco is an extremely well-run steel producer based in Hamilton, Ontario, that has delivered good results in a difficult industry environment. Lately the company's focus has been on cost cutting; lean and profitable is its prescription for the new millennium. Its product lines include hot-rolled, cold-rolled, and galvanized and tin-plated flat-rolled steels, as well as tubular products. Dofasco's wide range of steel products is sold to customers in the automotive, construction, steel distribution, packaging, pipe and tube, manufacturing, and appliance industries.

As part of a strategy to provide customers with global solutions, Dofasco Inc. and Sollac of France will be opening a new facility in Hamilton to produce advanced steel products for the North American automotive industry. Eighty percent of the joint venture is owned by Dofasco and 20 percent by Sollac, a subsidiary of Usinor

Group. DoSol Galva will be the first North American plant to produce hot-dipped galvanized steel for exposed automobile parts; it's a durable and cost-effective alternative to the electrogalvanized material currently in use. This alliance gives Dofasco's cornerstone Hamilton operation a competitive advantage by bringing new steel technology and production closer to where key purchasing decisions will be made, in an increasingly globalized and concentrated automotive industry.

In an era when everybody else seems to be bulking up to Arnold Schwarzenegger size through mergers and acquisitions, Dofasco president and chief executive officer John Mayberry intends to keep the company lean. Mr. Mayberry told a meeting of the Empire Club in Toronto that, in his view, bigger is not necessarily better. "To this I say, 'Investor beware,' and question how many of these mergers will deliver the intended strategic value," he declared.

Dofasco has spent its excess cash in aggressively upgrading its plants instead of chasing down mergers and acquisitions. This is a positive aspect in the view of both investors and financial analysts. "Dofasco has introduced a lot of cost reductions . . . and that could benefit the company when it comes to earnings growth," said Anna Sorbo, an analyst with CIBC World Markets Inc. As a result of these cost-cutting measures, Ms. Sorbo has a "buy" recommendation on the stock.

Ms. Sorbo also likes Dofasco because she expects to see a continued, gradual improvement in the price of steel. The price of commercial-grade hot-rolled steel has risen to around U.S.$300 a ton from about $250 in the first quarter of this year. This is the result of an improving Asian economy and tariffs imposed by Canada against some European countries, which have slowed the flow of imports into North America. As a result, the Toronto Stock Exchange Steels Index, after tumbling last summer, has been creeping up steadily over the past year, and Dofasco is leading the pack. The company's shares rose by about 38 percent in 1999, compared with a 26-percent return on the TSE Steels Index.

On an earnings-per-shipped-ton basis, Dofasco is currently North America's most profitable steel company. Dofasco's profit rose to Can$65.7 million, or 78 cents a share, for the second quarter of 1999, up from $56.8 million, or 66 cents, a year earlier. Sales climbed to $784.4 million from $741.3 million. Because Dofasco has strong cash flow — about $400 million a year for the past four years — but sees no significant acquisition prospects, it announced plans in mid-1999 to buy back up to 6.9 million shares, or approximately 10 percent of its public float, over the next 12 months. This is the company's second buyback in the past two years. A share buyback with cash flow makes the fewer remaining shares more valuable.

The costs of Dofasco's plant upgrades are expected to decline over the next few years, leaving the company with even more cash on hand. That's money that could be used either to buy back stock or to increase the dividends paid to shareholders. Most financial analysts agree that Dofasco is Canada's best-run steel company. They expect Dofasco's share price to rise gradually over the next 12 months as higher steel prices and the company's cost-cutting measures result in increased earnings over the long term.

My holdings of Dofasco total 159 shares, worth $3,679. I hope to buy more shares before the price moves too much higher.

DOFASCO INC. (DFS–TSE) www.dofasco.ca

Dividend Yield: 4.6%

Features of DRIP: One share required to enrol, with a $50 minimum purchase. No fees. Optional cash investment allowed, with quarterly minimum of $50 and annual maximum of $50,000.

How to Contact: CIBC Mellon Trust Company
Phone: 1-800-387-0825

Well Worth the Cost: National Bank of Canada

I debated for some time whether I should join the National Bank DRIP or not. National Bank had a very high initial minimum investment and also a high minimum for subsequent cash investments — in both cases, Can$500. This hurdle caused me to hesitate, but I decided that National Bank was quite undervalued. The major cloud over the company is the occasional outbreak of separatist fever in its home province of Quebec. But although the separatists generate noisy political debates, National Bank has built a strong franchise. And even a separate Quebec, after all, would need a bank. Sadly, it would then truly be the national bank.

My first shares were acquired for just over $10 each in 1995. By year-end 1995 I held 115 shares. The $500 minimum forced me to buy more than I would normally have purchased. My experience with National Bank has been as follows:

Year-End	Share Price	Shares Held
1995	$10.67	115
1996	$14.25	209
1997	$23.48	215
1998	$22.68	220
1999	$18.50	230
2000 (October)	$23.95	234

The high minimum turned out to work in my favour. Forced to buy more shares than I otherwise would have, I realized significant gains when the share price soared, doubling from 1995 to 1997.

How is the National Bank doing in its banking business?

- Actually, quite well in the most recent quarter. National Bank earned $133 million for the third quarter of 2000, up 25 percent from a year earlier. Looking at different types of earnings helps compare relative value among banks. High-value personal and commercial (P&C) bank earnings, combined with those from wealth management, typically account for 50 to 75 percent of a Canadian bank's earnings, and wholesale lines account for the balance. Historically, National Bank has been "P&C-strong."

- Savings are projected at $100 million over two years. Management are aiming for 8- to 9-percent cost savings from a variety of activities, including branch reconfiguration, process reengineering and centralization, and strategic sourcing contracts. National's branch reorganization program is meant to increase the number of point-of-sale outlets, but to reduce the square footage per branch.

- The bank, which is already the largest based in Quebec, has recently grown by adding brokerage firm First Marathon to its existing Lévesque Beaubien Geoffrion operation. This sends a signal that it wants to come out of the cold of Quebec and engage in more nation-wide operations.

My optimism regarding National Bank as a long-term investment continues. I now hold 242 shares, worth $5,709. New federal government rules for the financial services sector are likely to improve the value of National Bank's shares by allowing some bank mergers. It is even rumoured to be a takeover candidate. This is excellent news, as takeovers generally occur at higher share prices. I hope that, if the bank is taken over, the buyer continues the DRIP.

NATIONAL BANK OF CANADA (NA–TSE) www.nbc.ca

Dividend Yield: 3.23%

Features of DRIP: Minimum purchase of $500 and 100 shares required to enrol. (The $5,000 maximum presents few difficulties for the small investor, but a $500 minimum can be a barrier.) No fees.

How to Contact: National Bank
600 rue de La Gauchetière West
Montreal, Quebec H3B 4L3
Phone: 1-800-341-1419

A Successful Spinoff: NOVA Chemicals Corp.

NOVA Chemicals Corp. is a Canadian chemical company engaged in two principal businesses: the production of ethylene and a variety of chemical and energy products, and the production of styrene and styrenic polymers.

A company with enormous growth potential, NOVA Chemicals was spun off from a merger of the Alberta corporation NOVA and TransCanada PipeLines. The merger created a larger TransCanada PipeLines by adding NOVA's pipeline assets. It also created an independent NOVA Chemicals, focused entirely in the chemical industry. (At the time of the spinoff, NOVA shareholders received both NOVA Chemicals and TransCanada PipeLines shares.)

The company is moving its head office to the United States to be closer to its chemical industry customers. As well, NOVA Chemicals stands to benefit from two other important factors. First, the cyclical nature of the chemical business should produce much higher commodity prices over the next two to three years. Second, there is potential for a takeover of NOVA Chemicals as the overall industry consolidates.

For the three months ending in March 1999, revenues rose 9 percent over the same period the previous year, to $606 million. However, according to the U.S. GAAP (Generally Accepted Accounting Principles), net income fell 10 percent to $35 million. These results reflect higher sales volume, offset by lower margins due to lower prices. Nevertheless, NOVA looks to be poised for a rebound as chemical prices improve.

NOVA Chemicals pays a very small dividend of 40 cents per annum. It has a market capitalization of $2.1 billion and sales of $2.15 billion. My holdings include 149 shares of NOVA Chemicals, worth $4,327.

NOVA CHEMICALS CORP. (NCX–TSE; NCX–NYSE)
www.novachem.com

Dividend Yield: 1.4%

Features of DRIP: Minimum purchase of $50 per quarter; maximum of $5,000 per quarter. No fees.

How to Contact: CIBC Mellon Trust Company

Phone: 1-800-387-0825

Chapter 6

Land of Opportunity
My Favourite American DRIPs

The forty-ninth parallel divides the north american continent into two great nations, and I have had success investing south of it as well as north. American markets are larger and more volatile than Canadian ones. American equity investing is also more challenging in general because of the vast range of choices. DRIP investors have an advantage in this area, as the DRIP world is much smaller than the stock market as a whole.

It is not surprising that many investors have never heard of the small world of DRIPs and the advantages they provide. It is an unusual stockbroker who will recommend a stock program in which no commission is involved. Since no broker commission is paid on DRIPs, the virtues of these plans often go unsung. Only with shareowner investment clubs and, more recently, the Internet has this alternative to a broker-dominated investment world emerged into the mainstream.

DRIP investing in the United States makes sense for the same reasons that it does in Canada. Wall Street lives (some say feasts) on commissions paid by investors. Every purchase or sale of a share puts a few cents or more in the accounts of brokerage firms on Wall Street. Why put your hard-earned dollars in their pockets? As a direct investor you deal only with the company to which your investment dollars flow. In some cases you will deal with a trust company, as administrator for the plan, but you can say a fond farewell to the world of Wall Street commissions.

If you bought 100 shares of AFLAC, for example, through a full-service broker, your commissions could total several hundred dollars — dollars that come right out of your scarce investment funds. Even a discount broker is likely to charge you tens of dollars. But the AFLAC direct plan will charge you no fees for investing. You are ahead many investment dollars over the investor who uses a full-service broker. These are dollars that not only remain yours, but are also put to work as part of your investment. And with some DRIPs you get the additional advantage of a 5-percent discount.

The vast and booming U.S. market offers a veritable smorgasbord of DRIPs. Over the past seven years I have gradually built a portfolio of shares in American companies by investing in these plans. This portfolio is larger than my Canadian one, in fact, which is not surprising given the relative size of the two economies. At the time of writing, my U.S. portfolio contains 28 companies and a total of 2,389 shares with a market value of U.S.$87,000. These companies run the gamut of industries. Many, such as IBM, McDonald's, and Ford, need no introduction. Others, such as Philadelphia Suburban and New Century Energies, are more obscure (unless you happen to live in Philadelphia or Denver, Colorado). The list includes two burger chains, two banks, two insurers, and two utilities — a veritable Noah's ark of investments!

The American portfolio grew slowly in the first few years. I started by purchasing a single share in each of 10 companies. In July 1995 I held 423 shares in 16 companies, for a total value of $12,700. By October 1995 the portfolio had grown to 475 shares, worth $15,100. By May 1996 growth had accelerated to reach a value of $23,950, and by September the value had exceeded $27,000. The next phase marked even more rapid growth as I stepped up the pace of my savings. The market cooperated as well, producing price gains. By March 1997 there was a combined total of 1,344 shares, worth $42,590. Over the next two years the value of the holdings roughly doubled, even though the number of shares

My American Portfolio as of October 6, 2000 (U.S.$)

Company	Business	Shares Held	Market Value
AFLAC	insurance	344	$22,403
Atmos Energy	energy	172	$3,321
Central Maine	energy	111	$3,260
Diebold	ATMs	9	$225
Dow Chemical	chemicals	40	$1,055
Equitable Resources	oil and gas	103	$6,476
Ford	automobiles	31	$798
Hartford Financial	insurance	77	$5,557
Hannaford Brothers	food	22	$1,586
Huntington Bancshares	banking	164	$2,349
IBM	computers	4	$464
ITT Industries	manufacturing	118	$3,798
Johnson Controls	control systems	43	$2,378
Kerr McGee	resources	96	$6,163
La-Z-Boy	furniture	66	$891
McDonald's	fast food	159	$4,750
MediaOne	cable TV	47	$3,131
Exxon Mobil	oil	26	$2,325
New Century Energies	electric utility	166	$5,208
Philadelphia Suburban	water utility	71	$1,557
Reliant Energy	gas and electric utility	107	$4,753
Synovus	financial	110	$2,338
SBC	telecom	8	$426
Quest	telecom	171	$8,795
Visteon	auto parts	2	$35
Wendy's	fast food	29	$578
Wells Fargo	banking	73	$3,399
Whirlpool	appliances	17	$642
Total: 28 companies	**2,372 shares**		**U.S.$85,270** **(Can$127,905)**

increased by only 50 percent. Why? Higher share prices account for the lion's share of the jump in value.

My favourite U.S. DRIPs, not surprisingly, are mostly with those companies that have demonstrated terrific performance and that offer plans with good features. In most cases rapid corporate growth has produced spectacular stock-price performance and a great investment return. In a few other cases I just like owning a tiny part of the company, and look forward to future growth. There are also a few special situations where long-term trends are likely to transform slow-growth utilities into much more interesting investments.

Investment trends play an even more important role on the U.S. side of the DRIP world. Because there are so many more DRIPs available than in Canada, you need to make tougher selections. Investment trends or themes can help you with choosing the right DRIPs. Key trends south of the border currently include consolidation of the electric utility industry and consolidation of the financial sector. Another theme you'll note in my investment choices is food, glorious food; I think there's good potential in several areas of this sector. As in Canada, there are also some companies I chose because of their outstanding individual features rather than any particular industry trend. One of the true standouts in both pure investment and DRIP terms is AFLAC.

IN A CLASS OF ITS OWN: AFLAC

AFLAC is an American insurance company with a fast-growing niche: supplementary insurance. It specializes in medical insurance policies that cover specific conditions, primarily cancer. The company pays cash benefits either as a Medicare supplement or for intensive, long-term (nursing home), or in-home care.

Although based in the American state of Georgia, AFLAC has enjoyed phenomenal growth in Japan, where it is the leading cancer-expense insurance company and the largest foreign insurer of any kind in terms of both premium income and profits. In the U.S. it is the largest seller of supplemental insurance. Japanese sales are based on the agency system, in which a company forms a subsidiary to sell AFLAC's insurance to employees. In the U.S. the company also sells primarily through the workplace, with employers deducting premiums from paycheques. The total number of lives insured by AFLAC worldwide exceeds 40 million. Recently it has become much better known through its sponsorship of a television trivia quiz.

Andrew Leckey included AFLAC in his book *Global Investing 1999: A Guide to the 50 Best Stocks in the World*. He cites AFLAC's superior performance over the past decade: From 1990 to mid-2000, AFLAC's share price increased from $5.10 to $64.00 (adjusted for stock splits) — a great gain overall. In fact, if you had reinvested all your dividends, your compound annual rate of return would have been 29.9 percent. Happily, I did!

The table below shows how my investment of $3,800, made in small increments over six years, has grown through stock splits and dividends to a holding of 344 shares, worth over U.S.$22,000 or over $33,000 Canadian. My first shares were purchased one at a time in 1994 for $30 each. Those shares have since been split twice; a 1996 stock split yielded 43 new shares and another in 1998 brought me a further 169 shares. The original shares, adjusted for splits, cost me just $7.50 apiece. They are now worth over $64 each.

My AFLAC DRIP		
Year	*Investment*	*Shares Owned at Year-End*
1995	$1,700	80
1996	$700	144
1997	$400	153
1998	$1,000	341
1999	nil	342
2000 (September)	nil	344

My investment has increased in value by well over 500 percent. This is largely because of share-price appreciation, although dividends helped a little bit. The key element has been the continued stream of my investment dollars into the DRIP. The returns are excellent — the annual return of 29 percent results in a doubling in under three years. This performance is in the legendary, Warren Buffett category. Indeed, my success with AFLAC gives me some insight into why Mr. Buffett, America's greatest investor, likes *his* insurance company investment (GEICO) so much.

AFLAC (AFL–NYSE) www.aflac.com

Dividend Yield: 0.5%

Features of DRIP: Minimum initial investment of $1,000, paid by cheque, and a $50 minimum for subsequent investments. No other fees or charges.

How to Contact: AFLAC
1932 Wynnton Road
Columbus, Georgia 31999
U.S.A.
Phone: 1-800-235-2667

BANK CONSOLIDATION

Ever since the lifting of legislative restrictions that kept American banks from merging into large national banking organizations, the race has been in full flight. Luckily, I have two fast steeds for the course ahead. These two banks, Synovus and Huntington Bancshares, are both thoroughbreds with lots of potential to win the race.

Huntington Bancshares

Headquartered in Columbus, Ohio, Huntington Bancshares has exceptional banking expertise and has grown steadily through mergers. This growth has produced superior returns for its shareholders. (Companies with headquarters in cities named Columbus seem to be my lucky charm. Both Huntington and AFLAC are located in a Columbus, although in different states.)

The power of dividend reinvestment is well illustrated by my experience with this U.S. regional bank. My initial investment was not made until 1995, when I bought one share for $22. Over the next four years my holdings grew to 131 shares through investments of $2,600, stock splits, and dividend reinvestment. If I had invested earlier, the gains would have been even more dramatic. My gain of roughly 50 percent over less than four years is, nevertheless, excellent.

Reproduced on page 92 is a chart showing the 20-year track record of this acquisitive bank. Just $1,000 invested in 1988, after 10 years of dividend reinvestment, would have been worth $7,857 — a gain of 22.9 percent per annum. Huntington Bancshares investors have received cash dividends each year and many stock dividends, too. As well, over the past 20 years there have been no fewer than five stock splits.

Huntington Bancshares remains one of my favourite companies and one of my favourite DRIPs. This is because of their consistent ability to earn profits and, even more welcome, to share those profits with their shareholders. This is the type of performance that is most satisfying to the DRIP investor. Huntington truly makes your money work as hard as you work. My current holdings are 147 shares, worth $3,686.

HUNTINGTON BANCSHARES (HBAN–NYSE) www.huntington.com

Dividend Yield: 5.69%

Features of DRIP: Minimum initial purchase of one share. Additional cash investments allowed, with minimum of $200 per payment and maximum of $10,000 per quarter. No fees for reinvested dividends or optional cash payments.

How to Contact: Harris Trust
P.O. Box A3309
Chicago, Illinois 60690
U.S.A.

Huntington Bancshares Investment Record

Year	Cash Dividends (cents per share)	Stock Dividends	Stock Splits
1979	8	7%	-
1980	10	7%	-
1981	11	-	3 for 2
1982	13	10%	-
1983	13	10%	-
1984	15	10%	-
1985	17	-	2 for 1
1986	19	10%	-
1987	21	10%	-
1988	23	-	5 for 4
1989	25	15%	-
1990	29	10%	-
1991	33	5%	-
1992	36	-	5 for 4
1993	42	10%	-
1994	51	-	5 for 4
1995	56	5%	-
1996	62	10%	-
1997	68	10%	-
1998	76	10%	-
1999	80	10%	-

Synovus Financial Corp.

My second bank stock in the U.S. DRIP portfolio is another growth company. Synovus is a rapidly growing financial services company with over $11 billion of assets. It operates five business units, as follows:

  1. *Banking:* Synovus owns 36 banks, serving communities throughout Georgia, Alabama, Florida, and South Carolina. This company is building "the new bank" and expanding

its banking business by embracing change and investing in technology.

2. *Credit-card processing:* Synovus owns 80.7 percent of Total System Services Inc., one of the world's largest credit, debit, commercial, and private-label card processing companies.

3. *Trust services:* Holding more than $4.2 billion in client assets, Synovus Trust Company, a wholly owned subsidiary of Synovus Financial Corp., is one of the largest providers of trust services in the southeastern United States.

4. *Full-service brokerage:* Synovus Securities Inc., a wholly owned, full-service brokerage firm, provides investment services through 13 offices located in Georgia, Alabama, Florida, and Tennessee.

5. *Mortgage services:* Synovus Mortgage Corp. offers mortgage servicing throughout the southeastern United States.

Synovus has performed well for the last 10 years. Since 1988, when it began as a single bank, the company has been committed to superior customer service, conservative financial policies, and a decentralized, autonomous management approach. By allowing each affiliate company to retain its identity and culture, Synovus has gained great strength on the ground with its employees and customers.

My holdings of Synovus are modest. I bought my first share in 1994 for $18. Since then I have added to it through both direct investment and dividend reinvestment. I now own 109 shares, and the total value of my holdings is $2,935 — not bad on a total investment of under $1,000. Several share splits have helped me achieve the 100-share goal. I hope further growth and splits will assist with my 1,000-share goal.

SYNOVUS (SNV–NYSE) www.synovus.com

Dividend Yield: 2.07%

Features of DRIP: Minimum initial investment of $250, paid by cheque, and a $50 minimum for subsequent investments. No other fees or charges.

How to Contact: Boston EquiServe LP

Phone: 1-800-337-0896

WOULD YOU LIKE FRIES WITH THAT?

One of my favourite *Saturday Night Live* skits was John Belushi's hamburger stand. "Cheeseburger, cheeseburger, cheeseburger!" he would chant, followed by the recurring "No Coke! Pepsi!" There was an attractive maniacal energy about the routine — the samurai hamburger chef is sadly missed! The popularity of the skit showed how central fast-food burgers are to North American culture. They've become a mainstay of my portfolio, too.

McDonald's

McDonald's is just plain fun to own. Endlessly dragged to McDonald's restaurants by my children, I came to loathe the Happy Meals but to admire the business savvy behind their omnipresence. Once, after a week of exquisite cuisine at various chateaus in the south of France, I sought out a Big Mac — just to feel at home. It is comfort food supreme. Be warned, however, that the DRIP, like the restaurants, is *Mc*-intensive: The plan is called McDirect Shares!

McDonald's has 24,000 restaurants worldwide, with 50 percent, or just over 12,000 of them, in the United States. The company continues to grow in North America and around the world. We are all cooking less and taking out more; McDonald's will continue to benefit from this trend. Sheer scale also benefits McDonald's by supporting its strong global brand.

My first "McShare" was purchased in March 1995 for $34. I followed the initial share purchase by investing $200 in May 1995, which bought me 5.4 shares at $36.75, and a further $200 the next month, which added 5.3 shares at $37.73. The share price rose throughout 1995, and I kept buying. By November the price was up to $43.99. My first year as a McInvestor saw my holdings reach 36.67 shares — purchased with $3.81 of dividends and $1,400 of investment — which had escalated in value to $1,714.

For the next two years it was quiet on the McFront. I invested only $100 in 1996 and received four dividends totalling $8.65. By year-end the share price had dipped slightly; my investment was now worth $1,772. In 1997 I made one investment of $400 in August and received $8.83 of dividends. At year-end my investment was worth $2,140.

But in 1998 I became convinced that McDonald's shares were undervalued; growing sales and earnings were the deciding factor in my analysis. In keeping with my goal of reaching 100 shares, I made an investment of $2,000, which bought me 32 shares at $61.87 each. By year-end I owned 79 shares, worth $5,392. McDonald's shares continued to climb in 1999. By February my 79 shares were worth over $85 each, or U.S.$6,759 in total (over $10,000 Canadian). By August a split had allowed me to realize my 100-share goal; I now had 169 shares, still worth just under $7,000.

My cumulative investment in McDonalds amounted to $3,900; dividends accounted for small share additions. The vast majority of the gain was due to the rise in share price, from $36 to $85 over four years. Even with some recent softness in the share price, my investment has almost doubled in total value.

McDirect Shares now offers Internet access. You can obtain your account balance, dividend payment, stock price, and much more information on a secure Web site at http://gateway.equiserve.com. You need your account number, U.S. social security number (if applicable), and password for account access.

MCDONALD'S (MCD–NYSE) www.mcdonalds.com

Dividend Yield: 0.47%

Features of DRIP: Initial set-up fee of $5 and a $1 automatic investment fee. Commission of 10 cents per share bought or sold. Fee of $5 for optional cash purchases and a $10 sale fee.

How to Contact: EquiServe First Chicago Trust Division
Phone: 1-800-621-7825

Wendy's

I decided to pursue the burger investment theme further. In the wake of the success of McDonald's, I reasoned, there must be a Number Two who was trying harder. After some research, I decided that the best bet was Dave Thomas, and added Wendy's to the portfolio. A further deciding factor was the acquisition by Wendy's of the Tim Hortons doughnut chain. Tim Hortons was founded in Canada in 1964, and is the largest coffee and baked goods restaurant chain in the country. Hockey player Tim Horton lent his name to the business, but his untimely death meant that it was ex-policeman Ron Joyce who built the company to greatness. In fact, he continues to build the chain; the name on the door may be Tim Horton's, but the business genius behind the company is Ron Joyce. He has relentlessly expanded Tim Hortons, one outlet at a time, for 30 years. As a result of the merger, he is now Wendy's largest shareholder.

Wendy's is not quite as big as McDonald's, but with 4,297 franchised restaurants and 1,036 company-owned restaurants, it is not tiny either. Tim Hortons continues to generate record profits from its more than 1,700 outlets. Wendy's International Inc. is, in fact, one of the world's largest restaurant operating and franchising companies, with $6.5 billion in system-wide sales during 1998.

Wendy's International announced on September 20, 1999, that its board of directors had approved a $250-million increase to the company's share-repurchase program in order to buy back common stock over the next 18 to 24 months. (The company had at that point nearly completed, ahead of schedule, a $350-million repurchase program announced in 1998.) The repurchase of shares makes each remaining share more valuable. This is excellent news for Wendy's investors. The company believes it has ample financial capacity for the additional share repurchase while accommodating its growth initiatives and other strategic opportunities. The repurchase of shares is generally a positive sign for DRIP investors.

The company announced strong third-quarter 1999 sales trends at Wendy's U.S. and Tim Hortons Canada. This investment seems poised to head upward.

To date my Wendy's investment has been modest. I own 29 shares, worth $770. Over time, more of Wendy's will be mine.

WENDY'S (WEN–NYSE) www.wendys.com

Dividend Yield: 0.95%

Features of DRIP: Minimum monthly investment of $20 and a maximum of $20,000 per year. No other fees or charges.

How to Contact: American Stock Transfer Company
40 Wall Street
New York, NY 10005
U.S.A.
Phone: 1-718-921-8283

OIL'S WELL THAT ENDS WELL: EXXON MOBIL

In my student days I read Anthony Sampson's masterpiece, *The Seven Sisters: The Great Oil Companies and the World They Made*, on the world oil business. More recently I had the pleasure of reading Ron Chernow's extensive and captivating biography of John D. Rockefeller, titled *Titan*. Rockefeller was the founder of Standard Oil, which, when it was broken up, spawned no fewer than four of the "seven sisters" (Exxon, Mobil, Chevron, and British Petroleum). Given the global reach and massive scale of the oil business, I decided in 1995 to add one major oil company to each portfolio. My choice in Canada was the largest oil company, Imperial Oil, of which 70 percent is owned by Exxon, the successor to Standard Oil of New Jersey. (I discuss my experiences with Imperial Oil in Chapter 5.) For the American portfolio I selected Mobil, not wanting to put all my eggs in the Exxon basket.

With a history dating back to 1866, Mobil's energy and petrochemicals businesses today reach into some 140 countries. For 1998 its revenues were $53.5 billion and operating income was almost $2.4 billion. Investment spending reached $5.5 billion. Mobil's businesses are diversified as follows:

- *Upstream:* Mobil produces oil and natural gas in 20 countries and carries out exploration in 34. New projects enhance a strong position in liquefied natural gas.
- *Downstream:* Mobil's network of 23 refineries around the globe processes crude oil into fuels, lubricants, and petrochemical feed stocks. Mobil sells 3.4 million barrels of refined products a day in about 100 nations, in part through more than 15,000 Mobil-branded service stations.
- *Chemical:* Mobil Chemical manufactures and markets basic petrochemicals, additives and synthetics, catalysts, and flexible packaging films. The company operates 28 facilities and markets in more than 100 countries, with sales of more than 4 million tons in 1998.
- *Technology:* Through the partnership of Mobil Technology Company, Mobil seeks to reduce costs and create new products and growth opportunities for the other business units.

In 1999 Mobil and Exxon announced that they had reached an agreement to merge. Exxon shareholders would own about 70 percent and Mobil shareholders about 30 percent of the merged company, which would be renamed Exxon Mobil Corporation. Its headquarters would be in Irving, Texas, with worldwide downstream headquarters in Fairfax, Virginia, and worldwide upstream and chemical headquarters in Houston. For Exxon and Mobil to get their $82-billion merger approved, U.S. regulators required the sale of gasoline stations in the mid-Atlantic and northeastern states. The Mobil-Exxon merger was completed near the end of September 1999.

This merger has swept me back into the clutches of the Rockefeller empire — not a bad place to be as a shareholder. Post merger, it is likely to be not only the largest energy company on Earth, but the largest company of any kind as measured by revenue. With reserves and refining in virtually every major market in the world,

Exxon Mobil will be a secure bet — unless someone invents a perpetual motion machine. However, lingering legal residue from the 1989 *Exxon Valdez* Alaska oil spill is keeping the company in court as it fights the $5-billion fine levied by an Alaskan federal jury. Meanwhile, several companies in my Canadian portfolio, particularly Alberta Energy and Imperial Oil, provide me with some continued diversification in the sector.

My holdings of Exxon Mobil are modest, amounting to 26 shares, and worth $3,062. Clearly I am in no danger of overtaking the Rockefellers!

EXXON MOBIL (XOM–NYSE) www.exxon.mobil.com

Dividend Yield: 2.21%

Features of DRIP: Minimum initial investment of $250; $50 minimum monthly investment. No other investment fees. Sales fees of $5 plus 10 cents per share (relatively low for a company this size).

How to Contact: Phone: 1-800-252-1800

UTILITIES: A GREAT DRIP HOLDING

The gas company, electric utility, or local telephone company might not be your favourite company when their bills arrive each month. But, for an investor, this regularity has much to commend it. The safety of the revenues of utilities has long been a drawing card for investors. As I mentioned in the last chapter regarding my Canadian utility holdings, utilities have historically paid generous dividends and their share prices have reflected dividend yield more than growth prospects. There has been growth of demand for electricity and natural gas in recent years, but it has been slow and steady rather than explosive. Lately, however, many utilities are achieving remarkable growth in their earnings and share prices. Telecommunications was the first utility sector to undergo an acceleration in growth. That was due to new technologies, such as the mobile telephone and the advent of faster, cheaper long-distance service.

Now further change is underway in the sector. Competition is the new reality. Mergers and even hostile takeovers have come to this sleepy hollow of the North American economy. The American electric utility industry is in the early stages of consolidation. Utilities will combine to reduce their costs and to wire together larger electrical grids with millions more customers. Economics will come to dominate investment decisions. The electric utilities are following a trail already blazed by the gas utilities, which have been deregulated over the past several years.

New Century Energies/Xcel Energy Inc.

New Century Energies is one of the largest electricity and natural-gas companies (in geographic terms) in the United States, serving approximately four million people in the southwestern states. This investor-owned company traded under the NCE symbol on the New York Stock Exchange. After its pending merger with Northern States Power it will change its name to Xcel Energy Inc. and its symbol to XEL. Investors will receive 1.55 shares of XEL for every share they held of NCE.

New Century Energies has been busy with acquisitions. Now it includes the following operating companies: Public Service Company of Colorado; Southwestern Public Service Company; Cheyenne Light, Fuel and Power Company; and WestGas Interstate Inc. Other key subsidiaries include e prime, Natural Fuels, Quixx, Utility Engineering, and New Century International, which owns a 50-percent interest in Yorkshire Electricity Group PLC. In August 1995, the Public Service Company of Colorado merged with the Amarillo-based Southwestern Public Service Company and Cheyenne Light, Fuel and Power to form New Century Energies. This kind of lively merger activity is becoming the norm in utilities.

The new holding company has operating revenues of approximately $3.1 billion and serves more than 1.5 million electricity customers and 995,000 natural-gas customers. NCE employs approximately 6,300 people; its corporate headquarters is in Denver, Colorado.

The statement reproduced here from New Century Energies demonstrates an interesting benefit of DRIP investing. Note that on February 15, 1999, a dividend of $65.19 was credited to the account. This was a dividend of 58 cents per share on the 132.2241 shares then in the account; it was used to buy just a fraction over 1.5 shares. The share price in February was at $42.1875. In May the dividend, which is paid quarterly, bought 1.7 shares, and in August it bought just over 2 shares. Why? The share price declined from $42 to $38 to $33. Normally a decline in the share price would be a source of concern or disappointment. In DRIP investing the benefit is clear: Instead of 1.5 new shares for the third quarter, I received 2 new shares.

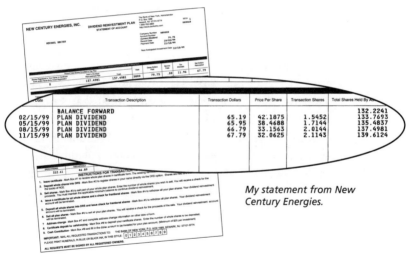

Date	Transaction Description	Transaction Dollars	Price Per Share	Transaction Shares	Total Shares Held By A...
	BALANCE FORWARD				132.2241
02/15/99	PLAN DIVIDEND	65.19	42.1875	1.5452	133.7693
05/15/99	PLAN DIVIDEND	65.95	38.4688	1.7144	135.4837
08/15/99	PLAN DIVIDEND	66.79	33.1563	2.0144	137.4981
11/15/99	PLAN DIVIDEND	67.79	32.0625	2.1143	139.6124

My statement from New Century Energies.

The company, my research tells me, is solid and growing. Accompanying my statement was the latest issue of *New Century Investor News*. Of particular importance is the company's pending merger with Northern States Power of Minneapolis — another example of merger mania in the utility sector. This merger has the potential to create a much larger and ultimately more valuable combined company. This is exactly the kind of news an investor likes to hear. As a shareholder, I hope the company's new name, Xcel, sets the tone and direction for my investment!

So why is the share price down? Who knows? The mutual-fund buyers who dominate the market may be bored with the New Century story or distracted by the latest Internet boom. There may also be increasing concern about inflation triggering a rise in interest rates. This normally reduces the share price for utilities, which, as a group, trade on their yields. When interest rates decline, the shares of utilities climb, and when interest rates increase, they decline. From my point of view I am delighted that the purchasing power of my dividend has improved. Better 2 shares four times a year than 1.5 shares. As the price goes back up, as I think it will, I'll have that much more gain in the long run. And DRIP investing, after all, is about the long run. So I will continue to accumulate New Century/Xcel shares until I retire.

It is also worth noting in the statement shown that my dividend increased ever so gently from $65.19 (February) to $65.95 (May) to $66.79 (August). This is caused by the additional shares in the account — really dividends on dividends, if you think about it. The new shares also receive the 58-cent dividend. Without any further investment, the account will grow steadily through dividends. Even at 8 shares per year, there will be a further 152 shares added to the 137 shares in my account by the time this 47-year-old reaches the age of 65. These 289 shares would generate over $670 per year in dividends, even without any further increases in the dividend rate.

My current holdings total 166 shares, with a value of $7,712. After the expected share exchange I will hold over 250 XEL shares, and I intend to buy further shares as my finances permit. New Century and its successor company have bright promise indeed as we move into the new century.

XCEL ENERGY INC. (XEL–NYSE) www.xcelenergy.com

Dividend Yield: 5.65%
Features of DRIP: Minimum cash investment of $50; set-up fee of $10.
Brokerage fees of 5 cents per share. Sales fee of $10.
How to Contact: Phone: 1-877-778-6786

Reliant Energy Inc.

Reliant Energy, or REI, is another company likely to benefit from industry consolidation. When I first invested, its name was Houston Industries. It has 3.6 million electricity and gas customers in the U.S. and also has investments in electric utilities in Argentina, Brazil, and Colombia that serve 3.3 million customers. The REI Retail Energy Group provides electricity to more than 1.5 million customers along the Texas Gulf Coast through Houston Lighting and Power; it also distributes gas to Arkansas, Louisiana, Minnesota, Mississippi, Oklahoma, and Texas. REI Trading and Transportation handles energy trading and marketing and also includes the company's gas-gathering and pipeline operations. The company's third group is REI Power Generation. REI's 1997 purchase of gas company NorAm doubled its sales.

I expect Reliant, which is based in Houston, Texas, to do well in the current acquisitions-mad climate for two reasons. First, it is already at a large enough scale to acquire; Reliant has $11.5 billion in annual revenue and assets of more than $19 billion. Second, it has established a growth track record already.

My holdings of Reliant Energy total 107 shares, worth $4,749. This compares to a total investment of $2,100 over six years — more than doubled! Reliant ranks as a solid investment.

RELIANT ENERGY INC. (REI–NYSE) www.reliantenergy.com

Dividend Yield: 3.69%
Features of DRIP: Minimum initial investment of $250. No fees.
Minimum cash purchase of $50.
How to Contact: Phone: 1-800-231-6406

WATER, WATER EVERYWHERE

Water, particularly clean water, is becoming a much more valuable commodity. Consumers and industries both use water, and some industries must obviously use lots of water. Think of Coke and Pepsi or Miller and Coors Brewing. How long would they survive without clean, drinkable water?

And yet neither would Intel. To make just one microchip as big as your fingernail, you need 150 gallons of sterilized water. You need even more water to make the computer that uses the microchips (the glass screens, plastic casings, and even the electrical cords that run to the outlet in the wall all require water for their manufacture).

If water became scarce, software and Internet stocks like Microsoft, Amazon.com, and Yahoo! would suffer. Without ready access to cheap microchips, fewer computers would get sold. Less demand for computers means fewer people on-line. And when that happens, who needs more software? Fewer people than Bill Gates and friends were counting on, that's for sure!

And would Ford, Chrysler, and GM shut down? You bet. Every car they make requires up to 40,000 gallons of water — and that's just to make the steel for the frame. To make each tire on those cars, you need another 518 gallons! In short, the worldwide demand for water is enormous.

A revolution is underway as new technologies for cleaning and purifying water are being developed. As well, local water utilities are the latest acquisition target for giant infrastructure companies such as Enron or Suez Lyonnaise des Eaux.

The value of water utilities will be unlocked as they are acquired. While you are waiting, dividend yields are often 3 to 4 percent. If you are lucky, the acquiring company will allow your DRIP to roll over into their DRIP. This was the case for me when Philadelphia Suburban acquired Consumers Water — read on!

Consumers Water Co. and Philadelphia Suburban Corp.

In 1996 I invested in Consumers Water, purchasing my first share for $17.35. Shortly thereafter, still in 1996, I purchased a further $300 worth — 17.29 shares. By the end of 1996 I had invested $700 and owned 42.78 shares. Since then I have not invested, but my dividends have purchased additional shares. In 1997 the four dividends added 2-plus shares to my total holdings. In 1998 dividends bought another 3 shares, and in 1999, before the takeover, another 2 shares.

The larger water utility Philadelphia Suburban made its takeover bid recently on a friendly basis. My holdings of Consumers Water became 70 shares of Philadelphia Suburban Corporation. PSC also announced an increase in its annual dividend rate from 68 cents to 72 cents per share. By June 2000, my holdings of PSC had grown to 71 shares, worth $2,122.

A summary of how my holdings grew is shown here.

Year	Shares	Value
1996	42	$752
1997	45	$844
1998	47	$1,466
1999	70	$1,685
2000 (June)	71	$2,122

Most of the growth in total value came from growth in the price of the shares, and a smaller amount from dividend reinvestment. If you had invested $100 in Philadelphia Suburban in 1994, it would have been worth $407 by 1998, a fourfold increase. That same $100, invested in the S&P 500 stock index, would have increased in value to only $294 over the same five years. Not too wet after all!

Philadelphia Suburban shareholders received a total return of 38 percent (stock price appreciation and dividends) in 1998, and a compounded annual shareholder return of 32 percent over the past five years — the best in the water utility industry. Not all water utilities outperformed the S&P 500, however. The Edward Jones Water Utility Index increased to only $244 over the same five-year period — less than the $294 of the S&P 500. Good water companies, like good water, require patience to locate. You need to use your investment divining rod: good research.

My own research, for example, suggests that Philadelphia Suburban Corp. continues to be a good bet. Its continuing cost-containment programs have produced higher profits while moderating water rates. Operating expenses have now decreased to 39 percent of revenues — one of the lowest in the industry — as a direct result of economies of scale resulting from its strategy of regional growth through acquisition. Consumers Water Co., serving approximately 225,000 customers, and with water and waste-water utilities across the eastern U.S., was its largest purchase so far. Its acquisition provided Philadelphia Suburban Corp. with growth and expansion opportunities both in the local Philadelphia Suburban Water Company (PSW) region and in new territories in five states. Under the merger agreement Consumers became a wholly owned subsidiary of Philadelphia Suburban Corp., making the company one of the largest investor-owned water utilities in the nation. The merger has taken place at a very dynamic time in the water utility industry, when there is significant opportunity for consolidation. The combination with Consumers represents a significant expansion of Philadelphia Suburban's regional growth-through-acquisition strategy. The regional growth and cost-containment strategies used at PSW are now being employed in Consumers' territories.

Philadelphia Suburban's aggressive acquisition strategy is beneficial not only to shareholders, but also to customers, as it provides economies of scale that result in decreased operating costs per customer, reasonable water rates, and superior customer service. In 1998, PSW was recognized in a Pennsylvania Public Utility Commission report as having the lowest customer-complaint ratio of any water utility in the state. According to its own annual report,

Philadelphia Suburban Corp. intends to build on its financial record by continuing to expand its water and waste-water businesses while also pursuing additional water-related opportunities.

PSC shows that water utilities represent an opportunity crying out for investment. A once-sleepy business with good dividends, water utilities are ripe for consolidation and new technologies to improve their efficiencies. I expect a massive consolidation of small water utilities into a few giant companies, as illustrated by PSC. Companies like Enron, a leading innovator among U.S. energy companies, will likely lead this parade, but other regional companies will also participate.

The stock of Philadelphia Suburban Corp. (PSC), which is the parent company of the Philadelphia Suburban Water Co. (PSW), is traded on the New York Stock Exchange. Approximately 60 percent of PSC's shareholders of record are customers of PSW. All PSW customers are eligible to buy stock directly from the company as part of their Dividend Reinvestment and Direct Stock Purchase Plan. This is an excellent sign.

PHILADELPHIA SUBURBAN CORP. (PSC–NYSE)
www.suburbanwater.com

Dividend Yield: 3.3%
Features of DRIP: No fees. Minimum initial purchase of $500. Minimum cash payment of $50. Dividends reinvested at a 5% discount.
How to Contact: Phone: 610-525-1400

ATMOS ENERGY CORP.

Atmos Energy Corporation distributes natural gas and propane to more than a million residential, commercial, industrial, and agricultural customers in 13 states. Based in Dallas, Texas, Atmos has expanded steadily and surely in recent years. My investment in it is yet another sign of my confidence in the trend of utilities enjoying dynamic growth.

Atmos's earnings were negatively affected in 1999 by warm weather and by heavy rainfall in West Texas, which decreased sales of natural gas for powering irrigation pumps. Earnings were also reduced by settlement of litigation in Louisiana. Atmos increased its quarterly dividend to 29 cents in November 2000.

This is the thirteenth consecutive annual dividend increase.

My holdings of Atmos Energy total 170 shares, which are worth $4,845. This is a gain from the $3,310 I invested between 1994 and 1998, but a modest gain. Atmos is an excellent example of a patient, buy-and-hold investment.

ATMOS ENERGY (ATO–NYSE) www.atmosenergy.com

Dividend Yield: 4.73%

Features of DRIP: Minimum initial investment of $100, paid by cheque. Minimum of $25 for subsequent investments; maximum of $100,000 per year. No other fees or charges (the company pays commissions).

How to Contact: BankBoston

c/o EquiServe

P.O. Box 9041

Boston, MA 02205-9835

U.S.A.

ITT INDUSTRIES

My holdings in ITT Industries (ITT–NYSE) originated with the breakup of the huge conglomerate ITT. One of the resulting smaller companies, ITT Industries is engaged in the design and manufacture of a wide range of engineered products, including connectors and switches, defence products and services, pumps and complementary products, and specialty products.

ITT describes itself as follows: "ITT Industries employs world-class engineers with a passion for engineering and manufacturing durable, reliable products. Our products and services meet vital human needs in growing global markets and create long term value." I like the breadth and depth of ITT's businesses. In a world that seems increasingly governed by the electron, this company still makes real stuff.

Four business units make up the company, as outlined below:

1. *Pumps and complementary products:* This business unit has a truly global presence, doing business in more than 130 countries. Pumps, valves, heat exchangers, mixers, and instruments are its key products. ITT's recent acquisition of Goulds Pumps resulted in cross-selling opportunities and operating synergies, and also led to a joint venture with Sinopec — the world's largest petrochemical company and single biggest user of process pumps — for the import and eventual manufacture of Goulds' chemical-process pumps in China.

2. *Defence products and services:* This business unit has employees in 27 countries and contracts in 29 countries. Its key products are digital communications systems, imaging and sounding instruments for weather satellites, radar systems for air traffic control, technical and support services for the U.S. military, night-vision equipment for military and commercial use, and airborne electronic warfare systems that protect aircraft from attack. This business unit has enjoyed six consecutive years of double-digit growth in international sales. It recently finished integrating Kaman Sciences, a 1997 acquisition that is a respected provider of advanced technical support services. ITT Industries' defence business ended 1998 with a $2.2-billion backlog of contract orders.

3. *Connectors and switches:* These products, which are sold around the world, include cable assemblies, switches, test accessories, I/O card kits, smart-card connectors, LAN components, and network systems and services. Three unique ITT connectors are on board both the Russian *Zarya* and the U.S. *Unity* modules of the international space station. They performed flawlessly as the first elements of the space station were launched into orbit. The switch business in mobile communications grew by 65 percent in 1998

through sales to accounts that included Nokia, Ericsson, Motorola, and Alcatel.

4. *Specialty products:* This unit has a presence in 10 countries. Its key products are fluid-carrying systems and tubing, specialty shock absorbers, brake friction materials, valves, switches, whirlpool pumps, submersible bilge pumps, and other recreational marine products. This unit has made several recent acquisitions, including Rule Industries Inc., a leading manufacturer of marine products that include submersible bilge pumps, anchors, and compasses; the U.K.-based Sinton Engineering Group; and Sweden's AG Johansons Metallfabrik AB, manufacturers of components for the pharmaceutical and bio-processing industries. This last acquisition bolsters ITT's presence in these robust European industries.

My 118 ITT Industries shares have a value of $5,624 as of June 30, 2000. This represents a gain of $2,100 from my original investment of $3,500 — not bad so far.

ITT INDUSTRIES (ITT–NYSE) www.itt.com

Dividend Yield: 1.75%

Features of DRIP: Minimum initial investment of $100, paid by cheque. Minimum of $50 and maximum of $120,000 for subsequent investments. No other fees or charges.

How to Contact: Bank of New York
P.O. Box 1958
Newark, NJ 07101-9774
U.S.A.

INVESTING IN BIG BLUE: IBM

IBM is the dominant manufacturer of mainframe computers, but the services business is now its most important — its ISSC division is a major contributor to overall corporate profits. Big Blue came back from a near-death experience in the early 1990s and has regained its spot as a favourite with small investors.

IBM (International Business Machines) is the world's top provider of computer hardware, software, and services. The company makes a broad range of computers, including desktop, mid-range, and mainframe computers and servers. Its peripheral products include printers and devices for networking, storage, and telecommunications. IBM also provides information technology services such as consulting and systems integration. Among its Internet operations is the on-line information service infoMarket. IBM also owns software pioneer Lotus, developer of the Lotus Notes messaging system. Nearly 60 percent of the company's sales are to foreign customers.

For DRIP investors, Big Blue is not a cheap date, although it has a $50-per-month plan that is not a bad way to go. Fees are high and dividends are small, but stock splits make up for these two negatives. I currently own a mere four shares of Big Blue. My intention is to add to my collection when IBM has a bad year or quarter that leads to a lower share price.

IBM (IBM–NYSE) www.ibm.com

Dividend Yield: 0.4%

Features of DRIP: Minimum initial investment of $500, paid by cheque, or $50 per month by automatic deduction. Minimum of $50 for subsequent investments. A fee of $1 plus commission for investments made through automated withdrawals from a bank account. Dividend reinvestment fee of 2 percent, to a maximum of $3. Initial account set-up fee is $15. A charge of $5 plus 2 percent for each optional share purchase, to a minimum of $3. A fee of $15 plus 10 cents per share commission for sale of shares through the plan.

How to Contact: First Chicago Trust

Phone: 1-888-426-6700

Chapter 7

Useful Resources for the DRIP Investor

THE INTERNET HAS CHANGED EVERYTHING, OR SOON WILL. Investing is no exception. In the very recent past, gaining access to DRIPs required significant effort, or joining a shareowners' association. Even with such an association membership there was quite a bit of paperwork involved. No longer — you can now request enrolment materials for hundreds of companies via the Net.

The Internet is not your only option. In both Canada and the United States shareowners' associations still offer access to many DRIPs. Some brokerage firms also offer automatic dividend reinvestment. You can avoid commissions on the reinvestment of dividends through these brokerage firms, but not the commissions on additional purchases. Still, lodging your DRIP portfolio with a discount broker is a reasonable option. All three of these options — do-it-yourself over the Internet, shareowner clubs, and discount brokers — are viable. And, of course, information about DRIPs and investing in general is available not only from many on-line sites but also through such traditional dead-tree sources as books, magazines, and newspapers.

WONDERFUL WEB SITES: INTERNET RESOURCES FOR DRIP INVESTING
As the Internet continues its spectacular growth, some terrific Web sites dedicated to assisting dividend reinvestment and direct investment have sprung up. You don't need to have a computer at home

to use this great resource; many public libraries can provide Internet access. So can a friend or a colleague at work. You can even visit one of many cyber cafés and log on for an hour while enjoying your latté.

The Web sites discussed below provide speedy access to information about thousands of companies with DRIPs, as well as further information about DRIPs and direct investing. You can usually request on-line the enrolment materials for a company's DRIP.

If serious investing is your goal then the best direct investing Web site is DRIP Central, located at www.dripcentral.com. In addition to lots of excellent analytical information, DRIP Central lives up to its name. The DRIP Central home page is reproduced below:

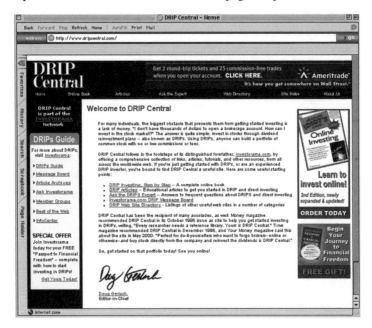

One Share

Among the most fun DRIP-related Web sites is the www.oneshare.com site, owned and operated by One Share of Stock Inc. This innovative company offers would-be shareowners the ability to buy an original share certificate — framed, if you wish. This could be an excellent way to start your one-share-at-a-time investing, especially if you want to involve your kids. You could dedicate a wall in your study or bedroom to the share certificates. Apparently the Disney certificate has Mickey, Pluto, and other characters adorning it. For $49 plus the actual cost of the share, One Share of Stock will frame and deliver to you a one-share certificate in any one of the companies on their list, including such notables as Disney, America Online (AOL), and Yahoo!

Shareowners' Associations

In Chapter 3 I discussed two extremely helpful starting points for DRIP investors: the Canadian Shareowners Association in Canada and the National Association of Investors Clubs in the United States. Both offer low-cost investing programs and can help you buy your first share of many corporations. Both also have informative Web sites:

National Association of Investors Clubs (NAIC)
www.better-investing.org

Canadian Shareowners Association (CSA)
www.shareowner.ca

The CSA's Low Cost Investing Program includes a broad spectrum of companies in Canada and the United States. Fifty-five companies are offered, ranging from Walt Disney to Gillette. The list is reproduced here.

Financials

AFLAC
Bank of Nova Scotia
Citigroup
Fairfax Financial
Imasco
Investors Group
National Bank
of Canada
Power Corporation
Royal Bank
Synovus Financial
Toronto-Dominion
Bank
Total System
Services
Trimark Financial

Consumer Products

Cinram
Colgate-Palmolive
Gillette
Home Depot
Loblaw Companies
Unican Security
Systems
Wal-Mart

Health Care

Abbott Laboratories
Biomet
Johnson & Johnson
MDS
Merck & Co.
Stryker

Communications

CanWest Global
Seagram Company
Teleglobe
Thomson
Walt Disney

Food and Beverages

Campbell Soup
Coca-Cola
Hershey Foods
Kellogg Company
McDonald's
PepsiCo
Sara Lee
Wendy's

Technology

General Electric
Gennum
Intel
JDS Uniphase
Lucent Technologies
Microsoft
Motorola
Nortel Networks

Transportation

Bombardier
Canadian Pacific

Resources

Barrick Gold
Imperial Oil

Utilities

Aliant
BCE
BCT.Telus
Caribbean Utilities

Frith Brothers Investments   www.frithbrothers.com

This investment banker offers information about alternative methods of corporate finance, including DRIPs and other continuous equity programs.

Power Investing with DRIPs   www.powerinvestdrips.com

Also available by calling 847-446-4406, *Power Investing* is a newsletter published by George Fisher. It is an educational publication containing broad investment knowledge and information, including a directory of over 1,000 DRIP companies.

MicroInvestor Web Guide   www.microinvestor.com
A guide for the small investor (those having less than $1,000 to invest). Provides information on personal finance, social security, retirement, 401(k) plans, financial planning, personal-finance magazines, low-cost mutual funds, dividend reinvestment programs, credit reporting agencies, discount brokerages, and hyperlinks to sites that specialize in providing information on the above items.

Mining Co.   www.miningco.com
This site's Stocks section provides a catalogue of links to DRIP resources.

The Motley Fool   www.fool.com
Information about DRIPs and a model DRIP portfolio are among the wide range of investor information and advice offered by the Fool. Among relevant topics covered at this popular site are these:
- What are DRIPs?
- Starting a DRIP
- History of DRIPs

The site also features message boards on DRIP investing — one for the basics and one dealing with specific companies. Message boards allow individual DRIP investors to share their stories, lessons, and experiences.

Yahoo! Finance   http://finance.yahoo.com
If you have access to the Internet, the Yahoo! Finance Web site will let you track the value of your DRIP portfolio on-line. There is no charge for this service. Simply go to Yahoo! Finance, then Stock Quotes. Select "Create Portfolio." You then need to name your portfolio (mine have the original names DRIP-US and DRIP-Canada). Then you need to enter your portfolio holdings. You'll need the

stock symbol, but don't panic if you don't know it. Yahoo! allows you to look it up. By entering the stock symbol plus the number of shares you own of each stock, you can complete the set-up of your portfolio. For more complete tracking, you can also enter your purchase price and date. Every time you buy more shares, simply update the information in Yahoo!

With these inputs, Yahoo! performs magic. It tracks the value of each stock in the portfolio as well as the portfolio's overall value. It also links you to all news about your companies on a real-time basis. For example, if you own shares in IBM and they announce a new computer, Yahoo! puts the press release at the bottom of your portfolio. You can also readily access research about companies, insider trading (buying and selling by company directors and managers), and other relevant information. One thing not tracked by this service is dividends. You'll need to enter any new shares purchased with dividends; this is easy to do, however.

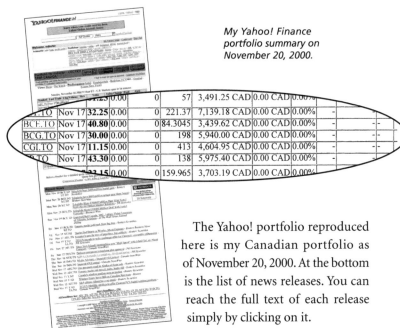

My Yahoo! Finance portfolio summary on November 20, 2000.

The Yahoo! portfolio reproduced here is my Canadian portfolio as of November 20, 2000. At the bottom is the list of news releases. You can reach the full text of each release simply by clicking on it.

Netstock www.netstock.com

Netstock offers several features on its Web site, including a database of 1,600 DRIP plans. As well, enrolment materials can be accessed and ordered here. As a free subscriber to Netstock.com, I receive messages like this one from August 31, 1999:

Dear Michael,

The last 30 days has been a very active time for Netstock.com as we continue to build a home for the direct investing community on the web.

First, our members are always looking for new companies to invest in and we're very pleased to announce that we have added 75 new plans administered by J.P. Morgan (a complete list is at the end of this mail). J.P. Morgan is one of the most highly respected firms in global finance and you'll see that reflected in the names they represent: companies like Sony, British Airways, Unilever, Reuters and many more. Netstock now provides online investment access to the majority of international companies offering direct investment.

Second, we've also added a number of other exciting companies to our online enrolment process. Names like Pfizer, Deere & Co, Unisource Energy, and CVS Corporation have joined our online group, now more than 325 companies in all.

Third, many of you have asked about retirement options so we've added IRA features to over a half-dozen of the current online plans. Today the list includes Wal-Mart, Fannie Mae, Allstate, American Electric Power, MCN Energy, SBC Communications, Ford and Campbell Soup.

Finally, our development team added a great new feature called "Quick Enrolment." If you've enrolled in an online plan before, we can now help you complete your next enrolment in three (3) screens. It makes you wonder what we all did before the advent of the Internet!

As we get ready to move into the fall season, we'll keep you posted on many more exciting additions to our direct investing house. Enjoy the rest of the summer season!

Best regards,

Jeff Seely
CEO, Netstock Direct
http://www.netstock.com

OTHER DRIP WEB SITES

The Public Register www.prars.com

From this site you can order free annual reports, or view them on-line, for thousands of DRIP and DSP (direct stock purchase) stocks.

DRIP Advisor www.dripadvisor.com

This site will help you take advantage of the exceptional returns in individual stocks by using DRIPs. It also provides the DRIP Investment Calculator to improve the returns on your DRIP investments by 15 to 25 percent over the long term. Another feature is the Research Zone, which allows specific company searches.

The DRIP Drop www.milliron.net/dripdrop

Each quarter, the *DRIP Drop* on-line magazine recommends five "momentum" picks. Questions about specific programs are answered as well.

BROKER SERVICES FOR DRIP INVESTORS

Several investment organizations provide help, and charge for their services.

Temper Enrollment Service www.moneypaper.com/enrolment

Temper Enrollment will buy shares in most U.S. listed companies with DRIPs, and it plans to extend that to all of them soon. Temper charges a service fee of $20 for each stock, plus a brokerage fee (50 cents for 1 share; $1 for 2 to 20; 5 cents each for 21 to 100 shares).

The service fee falls to $15 for subscribers to any of its investment publications or for members of its service, which for $49.50 a year gives access to *Direct Investing*, its on-line newsletter about DRIPs. Alternatively, investors can buy a one-day membership for $10 and still get the service-fee discount, which makes sense if you plan to buy at least three different stocks.

Phone: 1-800-295-2550

Web site: www.directinvesting.com

First Share

First Share Cooperative's Personal Portfolio Service will buy shares in any listed company its members request. That service will be attractive to investors who do not wish to be bothered with the record keeping required of most DRIP plans, because it will track each position on a comprehensive statement.

Phone: 1-800-683-0743

GOOD STUFF TO READ: A DRIP BIBLIOGRAPHY

Many publications offer excellent financial reporting and investment information. Here is a non-exhaustive list:

Periodicals

Canada
- the *Globe and Mail Report on Business* (daily)
- *National Post/Financial Post* (daily)
- *Canadian Business* magazine
- *Report on Business* magazine
- *Financial Post* magazine

United States
- *Forbes*
- *Barron's Weekly*
- *Business Week*
- *Fortune*
- *Wall Street Journal*

Here are two particularly relevant articles:

"Hunting Down a DRIP: Use the Web to find the best dividend reinvestment plans." *Money.* October 1998.

"About Dividend Reinvestment Plans." *USA Today.* January 30, 1998.

Books
American Association of Individual Investors. *The Individual Investor's Guide to Dividend Reinvestment Plans.* American Association of Individual Investors. The AAII is a membership organization that assists individuals in learning about all kinds of investments: bonds, stocks, mutual funds, annuities, etc.

Baryshnik, Jeff. *Fee-Free Investing: How to buy stocks and bonds and never pay a broker's fee.* Toronto: Doubleday Canada, 1999.

Carlson, Charles B. (Editor, *DRIP Investor*). *Buying Stocks without a Broker Using Dividend Reinvestment Plans.* New York: McGraw-Hill, November 1995. This paperback has sold over 150,000 copies to date.

Gerlach, Douglas ("the Armchair Millionaire"). *The DRIP Central Guide to DRIP Investing* [on-line]. www.dripcentral.ca.

——. *DRIP Investing, Step by Step* [on-line]. August 15, 2000. www.investorama.com/story/drips/dripguidecontents.

Tyson, Eric. *Investing for Dummies.* Foster City, CA: IDG Books Worldwide, October 1999.

Other Publications
Evergreen Enterprises publishes an annual guide to companies that offer DRIPs ($34.95 plus shipping). Contact them at 301-549-3939.

Chapter 8

More DRIPS to Investigate

THE COMPANIES THAT MAKE UP MY PORTFOLIOS ARE JUST THE tip of the iceberg of DRIP opportunities available to investors. In this chapter, I describe a number of companies in Canada, the United States, and abroad that I feel have good prospects, but that I have not invested in at this point.

BEYOND HOCKEY AND BEER:
MORE CANADIAN COMPANIES WITH DRIPS
Canada is blessed with a handful of well-financed and stable banks and a few dozen utilities of an impressive scale, as well as a range of other high-quality companies, some of which have the foresight and imagination to offer DRIPs.

Historically, the Toronto and Montreal stock exchanges listed most of the larger, better-funded companies in Canada, while the Vancouver Stock Exchange had an unsavoury reputation for "penny dreadfuls" such as mining stocks. However, a merger with several other small exchanges has transformed the Vancouver exchange into the CDNX exchange, which has a much better reputation to date as the venue for junior equity trading. Whether this is just the effect of a new coat of paint or a more profound change, only time will determine. The Montreal exchange now trades futures and options rather than stocks.

Companies offering DRIPs, as I've mentioned before, tend to

be among the better-established and well-financed enterprises on the market. The payment of dividends is a limiting criterion; many Canadian mining and oil companies do not pay dividends. Of course, paying a dividend is no guarantee of long-term business success, but it does mark a certain stability. Many of the most reliable dividend-paying companies in Canada are the utilities and banks — companies that offer DRIPs.

The following list is intended to be a starting place for more detailed research to help you launch a Canadian DRIP adventure of your own. (All dividend yields are calculated as of October 2000.)

Caldwell Partners International

Canada's leading executive search firm, Caldwell Partners, recruits executives for private- and public-sector organizations, and they have begun a business to provide temporary executives — Caldwell on Contract. Caldwell has a policy of paying out 80 percent of its earnings as dividends. Because employees of Caldwell are also shareholders, this policy is excellent for employee morale and motivation.

CALDWELL PARTNERS INTERNATIONAL (CWL–TSE)
www.caldwellpartners.com

Dividend Yield: 5.05%
Features of DRIP: A good, no-fee DRIP.
How to Contact: CIBC Mellon Trust Company
Phone: 1-800-378-0825
Web site: www.cibcmellon.ca

Molson Inc.

In the mood for a beer? Molson brews plenty of the golden beverage. The Molson Canadian jingle runs through every good Canadian memory bank at the mere mention of the name. After years of mediocre performance, Molson is changing as a company.

While Molson fiddled with side ventures such as ill-advised forays into home decoration, lumber, and chemicals, arch rival

Labatt turned the brew wars into a close horse race. The companies are now neck and neck with 45-percent market share. A decade ago, the gap was 13 percentage points in Molson's favour. However, there's well-founded reason for optimism that Molson is finally whipping itself into shape. Witness recent news: closing its Barrie plant, funnelling $100 million into its Toronto operations, and swallowing a one-time charge for restructuring of $188 million. Molson's team of executive brewmeisters is serious about getting back to the business of making suds and turning the 213-year-old company back into a cash cow. And none too soon.

Chief operating officer Dan O'Neill, who was hired in April 1999 to oversee the North American brewing operations, has impressed Bay Street with his resolve to make this old dog hunt again. He's been specific about numbers — closing a $100-million profit gap with rival Labatt, and within three years — a quality analysts love, especially given Molson's historical penchant for being not too focused.

The stock will do well if Molson follows through on its promises. The well-deserved skepticism means that Molson trades at a healthy discount — 20 percent or more on a price-earnings basis — to North America's other pure beer plays, Anheuser-Busch and Coors. While it's unlikely that gap will ever close entirely, it should narrow considerably once the efficiencies flow down to Molson's bottom line.

Molson's team is proving its mettle on the cost side. The next challenge is building market share. Key to that will be retooling (or exiting) its unproductive relationship with Miller Brewing, which imports and distributes Molson products in the United States. If it shows some growth in the import-mad U.S. market, Molson shares could really start hopping. And it has a great DRIP plan to go with that promising potential turnaround.

MOLSON INC. (MOL–TSE) www.molson.com/corporate

Dividend Yield: 2.8%
Features of DRIP: A one-share-to-start plan. No fees of any type. Minimum cash reinvestment of $100.

How to Contact: CIBC Mellon Trust Company
Phone: 1-800-387-0825

Canadian Bank DRIPs

The real money machines in Canada are the chartered banks, four of which offer DRIPs. My own portfolio includes the National Bank, but also well worth considering are the Bank of Montreal, CIBC, and Scotiabank. And when promised new federal legislation is in place, merger fever may once again grip Canadian banks.

The features of DRIPs for the Big Four are summarized below.

Canadian Bank DRIPs					
Bank	**Stock Symbol**	**Minimum Investment**	**Fees**	**Yield (Oct. 2000)**	**Contact Number**
Bank of Montreal	BMO	none	none	2.9%	1-800-332-0095
Bank of Nova Scotia	BNS	$100	none	2.6%	416-981-9633
CIBC	CM	$100	none	2.8%	1-800-387-0825
National Bank	NA	$500	none	3.2%	1-800-341-1419

All four of these Canadian chartered banks are traded on the Toronto Stock Exchange. The Bank of Montreal deserves particular attention. It is one of Canada's largest chartered banks. Although its well-known CEO Matt Barrett has departed for the helm of Barclays, new CEO Tony Comper is leading needed change.

There are several good reasons for selecting the Bank of Montreal as a DRIP investment. These include ongoing reductions in the expenses of the bank, increasing revenues from fees, and the possibility of future mergers. Each of these factors is likely to enhance the value of Bank of Montreal shares. Revenue growth is slow. However, expense cuts have started. Having fewer branches will free up capital in 2000 and beyond. The movement to electronic banking will allow the Bank of Montreal to earn more revenue with less bricks and mortar.

IPSCO Inc.

IPSCO is a steel producer based in Regina, Saskatchewan. Its main products include pipe for the major pipeline construction boom currently underway. Canadian natural gas is in high demand in U.S. markets, and IPSCO will benefit from the pipelines needed to be built to move gas from western Canada to American consumers. IPSCO's DRIP is a terrific no-fee plan.

IPSCO INC. (IPS–TSE) www.ipsco.com

Dividend Yield: 3.3%
Features of DRIP: Only one share required to enrol. No fees. Minimum monthly investment of $1; maximum quarterly investment of $5,000.
How to Contact: Montreal Trust Company of Canada
Phone: 1-888-334-3305

Nova Scotia Power

Electric utility Nova Scotia Power generates, buys, transmits, and distributes almost all the electrical power in Nova Scotia. It serves about 425,000 residential, commercial, and industrial customers. Nova Scotia Power also provides energy management plans to help commercial and industrial customers reduce energy expenses. Its subsidiary Nova Scotia Power Services Ltd. (PSL) designs, implements, and invests in energy projects for commercial, industrial, and institutional customers. PSL also provides engineering and management consulting services to clients in both local and international markets. Engaged in the production and sale of electricity since 1912, Nova Scotia Power was privatized in 1992. Nova Scotia Power is a slow-growth company, but its DRIP is a good one.

NOVA SCOTIA POWER (NSH–TSE) www.nspower.ca

Dividend Yield: 5.0%

Features of DRIP: Only one share required to enrol. No fees.

How to Contact: Montreal Trust Company of Canada

Phone: 1-800-561-0934

Additional Canadian Companies with DRIPs

The companies described above are good places to start if you're looking for DRIP portfolio prospects. I've done a bit of initial research for you and found they show some promise. Now, for those ready to do a bit more digging, here are the bare-bones stats on a few more Canadian companies that offer DRIPs. Why not put your research and analysis skills to work together with my investment tradecraft rules by checking some of them out? One may be the perfect start for your DRIP portfolio. But be sure to do your homework before deciding!

More Canadian Companies with DRIPs

Company	Business	Dividend Yield	Discount	Min.	Max.	Frequency
MDS Health	health services	0.29%	5%	$50	$3,000	SA
INCO	nickel	0%	0%	$50	$14,000	M
Alcan	aluminum	1.93%	0%	$100	$12,000	M
Westcoast Energy	pipelines	4.53%	0%	$50	$45,000	Q
Moore	business forms	6.97%	0%	$50	$5,000	Q
Suncor Energy	tar sands	1.03%	0%	$100	$5,000	Q

Frequency codes: M = monthly; Q = quarterly; SA = semi-annually

Trust Units: A Piece of the Sectoral Action

In addition to companies, there are also trust units that offer a reinvestment feature. These trusts cover several resource sectors such

Some Canadian Trust Units with DRIPs

Trust	Contact Number
Amalgamated Income LP	1-888-708-5757
Arc Energy Trust	416-981-9633
Athabasca Oil Sands	416-981-9633
CPL Long Term Care	1-800-387-0825
Canadian Real Estate Investment	1-800-387-0825
Enermark Income Fund	1-800-387-0825
Enerplus Resources Fund	1-800-387-0825
First Premium Income Fund	416-981-9633
NAL Oil and Gas	1-800-332-0095
NCE Energy Trust	416-364-8788
NCE Petrofund	416-981-9633
New Altamira Value Fund	416-981-9633
Pengrowth Gas Income	1-800-332-0095
Polar Hedge Enhanced IT	416-367-4364
Prime West Energy Trust	1-800-332-0095
Riocan Real Estate Investment	1-800-387-0830
Summit Real Estate Investment	1-800-387-0825
Templeton Emerging Markets Appreciation Fund	1-800-387-0830
Triax Diversified High Yield	416-362-2929
Wardley China Investment	1-888-661-5566

as oil and gas, oil sands, and real estate. They are well worth researching and considering for your portfolio. (My own experience with two energy-based investment trusts, Enerplus and Enermark, is described in Chapter 5.)

YANKEE DOODLE DANDIES: MORE AMERICAN COMPANIES WITH DRIPS

The great news is that a large number and wide variety of American companies have DRIPs. As in Canada, the companies offering DRIPs are usually larger, better established, and well-financed enterprises.

The simple requirement that DRIPs can be offered only by companies that actually pay dividends is an effective screening device. Many of the most reliable dividend-paying companies are the same companies that offer DRIPs to their shareholders. For example, Atmos Energy declared its sixty-sixth consecutive dividend to be paid June 12, 2000. Many other DRIP companies have been paying consecutive dividends for decades.

The exact number of American corporations offering DRIPS is hard to determine at any given time, but estimates range between 900 and 1,000. Chapter 6 detailed my own U.S. portfolio; here, I've supplied some basic company background and plan information on a number of other popular company plans. All dividend yields are calculated as of October 11, 2000.

Wal-Mart Stores Inc.

Wal-Mart is the world's largest retailer, operating more than 3,400 Wal-Mart stores, Sam's Clubs, and Wal-Mart Supercenters around the world. Wal-Mart competes with such discount retail chains as Kmart and Dayton Hudson's Target stores, as well as innumerable mom-and-pop variety and hardware stores. In the U.S. the company is upgrading operations, primarily by converting older, smaller Wal-Mart outlets into Supercenters.

WAL-MART STORES INC. (WAL–NYSE) www.walmart.com

Dividend Yield: 0.38%

Features of DRIP: Minimum initial investment of $250, paid by cheque, or $25 per month by automatic deduction. Minimum of $50 for subsequent investments. A fee of $1, plus commission of 10 cents per share, for investments made through automated deductions from a bank account. Initial account set-up fee of $20. Commission of 10 cents per share for each optional share purchase. Fee of $20 for sale of shares through the plan.

How to Contact: EquiServe First Chicago Trust Division
Phone: 1-800-438-6278

Fannie Mae

Fannie Mae's mission is to help the American dream of home own-ership come true for more families. Fannie Mae provides financial products and services that increase the availability and affordability of housing for low-, moderate-, and middle-income Americans. The corporation is the nation's largest source of home mortgage funds. This company is a long-time favourite of investment guru Peter Lynch. The Fannie Mae DRIP is relatively affordable and has a wonderful long-term track record.

FANNIE MAE (FNM–NYSE) www.fanniemae.com

Dividend Yield: 1.60%
Features of DRIP: Minimum initial investment of $250, or $25 a month for 12 months. Minimum of $25 for subsequent investment. Initial set-up fee of $15. Automatic investment fee of $2. Optional cash purchase fee of $5 plus 3 cents per share. Sales fee of $15, plus commission of 12 cents per share.
How to Contact: EquiServe First Chicago Trust Division
Phone: 1-888-BUY-FANNIE

Aetna Inc.

Aetna provides health and retirement benefit plans and financial services through Aetna U.S. Health Care, Aetna Retirement Services, and Aetna International. The company has been struggling since acquiring U.S. Health Care, and the future for Aetna rests upon better management of its health business.

I have had two encounters of a close kind with Aetna. For a period of time I served as a member of their Health Care Advisory Board in Canada. As well, APM Inc., the health-care consultancy where I worked, advised Aetna on their acquisition of U.S. Health Care in the mid-1990s.

Aetna's DRIP is at the middle to high end of the fee range, with a modest dividend. The company has the scale to persist in the insurance and managed-care industries.

AETNA INC. (AET–NYSE) www.aetna.com

Dividend Yield: 1.31%

Features of DRIP: Minimum initial investment of $500, paid by cheque, or $50 per month for 10 months. Initial set-up fee of $10. Automatic investment fee of $1, plus $5 for the cash investment option, and 3 cents per share. Sales fee of $15 plus 10 cents.

How to Contact: EquiServe First Chicago Trust Division

Phone: 1-800-446-2617

Mattel

Mattel is the number-one U.S. toy maker. The company's major brands include Barbie, Fisher-Price, Disney entertainment lines, Hot Wheels and Matchbox cars, and Cabbage Patch Kids. Its games include Skip-Bo and UNO. Mattel believes that children everywhere like the same toys, so it designs products with worldwide appeal and markets them globally. It sells toys in more than 140 countries, and about one-third of its revenues come from outside the U.S. Most of Mattel's sales stem from toys targeted to girls (led by Barbie), though the company is expanding its line of toys for boys. The company's primary manufacturing facilities are in the U.S., China, Indonesia, Italy, Malaysia, and Mexico. Mattel's DRIP is a reasonable plan, and great for kids. Will the boomers buy toys for their grandchildren? Mattel has a terrific Web site with an on-line store!

MATTEL (MAT–NYSE) www.mattel.com

Dividend Yield: 3.03%

Features of DRIP: Minimum initial investment of $500, paid by cheque, or $100 per month by automatic deduction. A $100 minimum for subsequent investments. Fee of $1 plus commission for investments made through automated deductions from a bank account. Initial account set-up fee of $10. A $5 charge for each optional share purchase, as well as commission of 8 cents per share. A $10 fee plus commission of 8 cents per share on sale of shares through the plan.

How to Contact: Phone: 1-888-909-9922

Walt Disney Co.

The Walt Disney Company has interests in TV and movie production (including Buena Vista Television, Miramax Film Corp., and Touchstone Pictures), theme parks (including Disneyland, Disneyland Paris, Epcot Center, and North America's most-visited theme park, the Magic Kingdom), publishing companies (Disney Press, Hyperion Press, and Mouse Works), and a professional sports franchise (the Anaheim Mighty Ducks hockey team). Disney's ABC Inc. division includes the ABC TV network, several dozen TV stations, and shares in five cable channels, including ESPN. The fees for Disney's DRIP are towards the high end of the range, but not totally goofy.

WALT DISNEY CO. (DIS–NYSE) www.disney.com

Dividend Yield: 0.51%

Features of DRIP: Minimum initial investment of $1,000, paid by cheque, or $100 per month by automatic deduction. A $100 minimum for subsequent investments. Fee of $1 plus commission for investments made through automated deductions from a bank account. Initial account set-up fee of $15. A $5 charge as well as commission of 3 cents per share for each optional share purchase. Fee of $10 plus commission of 3 cents per share on sale of shares through the plan.

How to Contact: Walt Disney Co.
500 South Buena Vista Street
Burbank, California 91521
U.S.A.
Phone: 1-800-948-2222

Intel

Intel is the world's number-one maker of microprocessors, with 90 percent of the market. Its microprocessors — including the Pentium chip — have been providing the brains for IBM-compatible PCs since 1981. The company also makes computer flash-memory chips, microcontrollers, networking products, and videoconferencing systems. In an effort to move into the graphics chip market, Intel recently acquired Chips & Technology. Intel continues to expand and upgrade its products and facilities to maintain its dominance over rival chipmakers such as Cyrix and Advanced Micro Devices. The company has plants in Ireland, Israel, Malaysia, the Philippines, and the U.S. Nearly 60 percent of its sales are outside the U.S. Lately, Advanced Micro Devices have been challenging Intel's historic dominance. No fees make Intel's DRIP a very low-cost plan. The dividends are very modest; this is a growth play, not a dividend play.

INTEL (INTC-NASDAQ) www.intel.com

Dividend Yield: 0.16%
Features of DRIP: Minimum initial investment is one share. Minimum of $25 for subsequent investments. No initial account set-up fee.
How to Contact: Harris Trust and Savings Bank
Phone: 1-800-298-0146

Ford Motor Company

One of the world's largest manufacturers of motor vehicles and related businesses, the Ford Motor Company was founded by American industrialist Henry Ford. His descendants are still active in the company's management. Ford's DRIP has a very high initial investment ($1,000). However, the $100-per-month plan eases the burden considerably. One of the unusual benefits of the Ford program is that you are able to take out a loan or establish a line of credit backed by the Ford common stock in your account.

FORD MOTOR COMPANY (F–NYSE) www.ford.com

Dividend Yield: 4.42%
Features of DRIP: Minimum initial investment of $1,000, paid by cheque, or $100 per month by automatic deduction. A $50 minimum for subsequent investments. Fee of $1 plus commission for investments made through automated deductions from a bank account. Annual

maximum of $250,000. Initial account set-up fee of $10. A $5 charge
as well as commission of 3 cents per share for each optional share
purchase. Fee of $5 plus commission of 12 cents per share on sale
of shares through the plan.

How to Contact: DirectSERVICE Program
Ford Shareholder Services Group
c/o First Chicago Trust Company
P.O. Box 2598
Jersey City, NJ 07303-2598
U.S.A.
Phone: 1-800-279-1237 (Canada and United States)
201-324-0272 (elsewhere)
E-mail: Ford_Team@em.fcnbd.com

Some Additional U.S. Companies with DRIPs

The companies discussed above are a few of the better known ones
that offer DRIPs. I've done the first steps of corporate and plan
research for you, but you'll want to do more, and think carefully
before making a final investment decision. You may also want to
check out some of the 900 or so other U.S. companies that offer
DRIPs — remember that an obscure company can sometimes be a
fine investment. I've listed a number of good, solid companies on
the next page to get you started. Good luck!

THE FOREIGN LEGION: COMPANIES OUTSIDE
NORTH AMERICA WITH DRIPS

It's a big world. There are excellent companies in Europe, Japan,
and elsewhere. Fortunately, many of them now offer DRIPs, so an
investor willing to look a little farther afield can take advantage of
their prospects.

Investing in DRIPs outside North America is greatly assisted by
the existence of American Drawing Rights, or ADRs. These certificates, issued in the United States, represent shares of companies
whose shares trade on stock exchanges outside North America.

More U.S. Companies with DRIPs

Company : business	Company: business
Amoco: oil and gas	Bankers Trust: bank
Bausch & Lomb: optical products	Banknorth Group: bank
Baxter Int.: medical devices	Bell Atlantic: telecom
Bay State Gas: utility	Bob Evans Farms: food
BEC Energy: energy	Comsat: technology
Beckman Coulter: instruments	Enron: energy
Becton, Dickinson: medical	First USA: financial services
BellSouth: telco	J.C. Penney: retailer
Benetton Group: clothing	Minnesota Light: utility
Berkshire Energy: energy	Oklahoma Light: utility
Bestfoods: food	Owens Corning: ceramics and glass
Bethlehem Steel: steel	Procter and Gamble: consumer goods
BF Goodrich: tires	Qwest: telecommunications
Birmingham Steel: steel	Readers Digest: publisher
Black & Decker: tools	Sears Roebuck: retailer
Baker Hughes: manufacturing	Texaco: oil and gas
Ball Corporation: manufacturing	TysonFoods: chickens (lots of chickens)
Baltimore Gas: utility	Wisconsin Energy: energy
Bank One: bank	
BankAmerica: bank	
BankBoston: bank	

ADRs trade in North America, allowing U.S. and Canadian residents to participate easily in foreign companies. Many foreign firms with familiar names such as Sony, Nokia, Royal Dutch Shell, and British Airways offer DRIPs.

There is even a dedicated Web site with information about ADRs, operated by the venerable bank J.P. Morgan; the site can be found at www.adr.com. It contains a search engine that allows you to seek ADRs across a variety of countries and industries. As well, analyst recommendations, earnings estimates, quotes, and other background information are accessible from this source. The New York Stock Exchange Web site (www.nyse.com) offers information on ADRs that are listed on the New York exchange.

As in North America, the foreign companies offering DRIPs tend to be the better-established and -financed enterprises. This is not always the case, however; always research a company thoroughly prior to investing. As in Canada and the U.S., many of the most reliable dividend-paying companies in the rest of the world are the same ones that offer DRIPs to their shareholders. These include some very familiar names such as Barclays Bank, Benetton Group, and ING, as well as many others that are widely known only in their countries of origin.

The combination of ADRs and DRIPs opens the broader world to the individual small investor. There are both benefits and risks in this opportunity. To assist those brave enough to consider the "foreign legion" of investments, I've included basic corporate and plan information on a handful of my top picks from among the hundreds of possible foreign companies. I don't yet have a portfolio of foreign DRIPs myself, but I intend to start one when I have reached my goal of 100 shares of each of the companies in my American and Canadian portfolios. Barring any unforeseen events, the companies discussed below will be the first stocks I buy in that new portfolio. My goal will be to acquire 10 shares of each company in the first year.

At the end of this book I've included an appendix containing a much longer list of foreign stocks with DRIPs, which you can use as a starting point for your own research. All of these companies trade ADRs on American stock exchanges.

International DRIPs generally involve higher fees than American or Canadian ones. Typical fees, which are usually applied to trust-company or bank-sponsored DRIPs, are as follows:

- initial account set-up fee $15
- optional cash investment fee $5
- commissions   12 cents per share

- automatic investment fee $15 plus 2.5%–5%
  of dividend amount
- sales fee $5

International DRIP plans also tend to have fairly high initial investment requirements, from $250 to $500 per company. Finally, dividend yields in the foreign legion are somewhat lower, on average, than in my American and Canadian portfolios. In my view, however, the opportunity to invest in truly global companies offsets these disadvantages.

The DRIP Central Web site (reviewed in Chapter 7) is a good place to undertake research on these companies and to link to their own Web sites for detailed information on their DRIP plans.

Sony

Sony is a complex corporation, and Japan's consumer electronics leader is a household brand name all over the globe. Led by the late dynamo Akio Morito, Sony emerged from the ruins of post-war Japan and took on the world in less than a generation. It is a global leader in innovative consumer products — think about the Walkman, the Watchman, and others. Now high-definition television, or HDTV, is the next big thing. Sony is positioned to lead a movement likely to render every existing television on the planet obsolete — and render large profits to Sony! Its business domain extends beyond electronics (both audio and video) to include games, music, pictures, insurance, information and communications, and more. The complete list of Sony products is staggering; see the Web sites for an idea of what I mean (Sony Online World: www.world.sony.com; Sony Online USA: www.sony.com). Sony's Web sites also offer a wealth of corporate and product information, including the latest annual report and financial results. Although the shares have run up in price lately, Sony is a great buy for the new century.

SONY (SNE) www.sony.com

Dividend Yield: 0.24%

Features of DRIP: Minimum initial investment of $250 and a $50 minimum for subsequent investments. Initial account set-up fee of $5. A $5 charge as well as commission of 12 cents per share for each optional share purchase. Fee of $5 for sale of shares through the plan.

How to Contact: Morgan Guaranty Trust

P.O. Box 9073

Boston, MA 02205-9948

U.S.A.

ING

This financial giant first came to the notice of global investors in the wake of the collapse of Barings Bank. The venerable Barings was done in by a single rogue trader, Nick Leeson, who vaporized the bank's equity in a series of catastrophic trades on the Tokyo stock market. ING bought the remains of Barings, adding it to an expanding global network of banks, investment banks, and insurance companies. Properly called ING Groep NV, this global financial institution is of Dutch origin (the head office is in Amsterdam). The company is active in the fields of banking, insurance, and asset management in some 60 countries. ING has a market capitalization of $53.9 billion, and it has been acquiring other financial companies at a steady pace.

I was impressed with the way in which ING entered the Canadian market. A bank without branches, it offered a terrific interest rate and simple, direct service. ING is an excellent company for the new millennium, and the ING DRIP has reasonable features.

ING (ING–NYSE) www.ing.com

Dividend Yield: 2.27%

Features of DRIP: Minimum initial investment of $250 and a $50 minimum for subsequent investments. Initial account set-up fee of $5. A $5 charge plus commission of 12 cents per share for each optional share purchase. Fee of $5 for sale of shares through the plan.

How to Contact: Morgan Guaranty Trust

P.O. Box 9073

Boston, MA 02205-9948

U.S.A.

Barclays Bank

One very good reason for considering Barclays Bank is its new CEO, Matthew Barrett. In his decade as CEO of the Bank of Montreal, Matthew Barrett transformed that institution from Sleepy Hollow to an innovator and leader among the Canadian banks. There are several other excellent reasons for considering Barclays, including the dividend (2.63 percent), the prospect of a turnaround, and the value of the franchise at a time of consolidation in global banking.

BARCLAYS BANK (BCS–NYSE) www.barclays.com

Dividend Yield: 2.63%

Features of DRIP: Minimum initial investment of $250 and $50 minimum for subsequent investments. Initial account set-up fee of $5. A $5 charge plus commission of 12 cents per share for each optional share purchase. Fee of $5 for sale of shares through the plan.

How to Contact: Morgan Guaranty Trust

P.O. Box 9073

Boston, MA 02205-9948

U.S.A.

Diageo PLC

Diageo was formed in the late '90s by a merger of the brewing giant Guinness and Grand Metropolitan PLC, a British food and beverage conglomerate. Grand Met includes among its companies the "other" hamburger restaurant chain — Burger King! It also owns a few other food businesses with valuable brands, including Pillsbury, Häagen-Dazs, and Smirnoff. The company's current, unusually high dividend is likely to decline. Its DRIP offers more burgers and fries, but you'll have to spend some fees to get them.

DIAGEO PLC (DEO–NYSE) www.diageo.com

Dividend Yield: 9.01%
Features of DRIP: Minimum initial investment of $250 and a $50 minimum for subsequent investments. Initial account set-up fee of $5. A $5 charge plus commission of 12 cents per share for each optional share purchase. Fee of $5 for sale of shares through the plan.
How to Contact: Morgan Guaranty Trust
P.O. Box 9073
Boston, MA 02205-9948
U.S.A.

Rank Group PLY

The Rank Group is a major entertainment group based in the United Kingdom. Among its diversified assets are the Hard Rock Cafes, a chain of pubs, restaurants, hotels, and an extensive film business. In total, nearly $3 billion in revenue will flow into Rank's coffers this year.

RANK GROUP PLY (RANKY–NASDAQ) www.rank.com

Dividend Yield: 5.27%
Features of DRIP: Minimum initial investment of $250 and a $50 for subsequent investments. Initial account set-up fee of $5. A $5 charge plus commission of 12 cents per share for each optional share purchase. Fee of $5 for sale of shares through the plan.
How to Contact: Morgan Guaranty Trust
P.O. Box 9073
Boston, MA 02205-9948
U.S.A.

Nokia

Nokia's cell phones have transformed not just the company but the entire nation of Finland, which it calls home. A global giant of the mobile phone and related businesses, which are on the rise world-wide, Nokia will earn over $21 billion in revenue. The company dominates the Finnish stock market in Helsinki the same way that Nortel Networks dominates the Toronto Stock Exchange. Both have core holdings in the new economy for the twenty-first century.

NOKIA (NOK–NYSE) www.nokia.com

Dividend Yield: 0.55%

Features of DRIP: Minimum initial investment of $250 and a $50 minimum for subsequent investments. Initial account set-up fee of $5. A $5 charge plus commission of 12 cents per share for each optional share purchase. Fee of $5 for sale of shares through the plan.

How to Contact: Morgan Guaranty Trust
P.O. Box 9073
Boston, MA 02205-9948
U.S.A.

Reuters

Reuters, which is based in the United Kingdom, is one of the oldest and best-known news services in the world. In addition to being a general news agency, Reuters is also a prominent distributor of financial information. It provides real-time financial data, transaction systems, access to numerical and text databases, news, photos, and video news to the news media and to the global business community. The Reuters Instinet unit offers traders the opportunity to deal in futures, foreign exchange, securities, and other markets from their desktop PCs. The company operates in 161 countries and relays news and financial information from over 360,000 computer terminals. Reuters has found the transition to the Internet world a challenge. However, it seems to be winning in its battle with chief rival Bloomberg.

REUTERS (RTRSY–NASDAQ) www.reuters.com

Dividend Yield: 0.69%

Features of DRIP: Minimum initial investment of $250 and a $50 minimum for subsequent investments. Initial account set-up fee is $5. A $5 charge plus commission of 12 cents per share for each optional share purchase. Fee of $5 for sale of shares through the plan.

How to Contact: Morgan Guaranty Trust
P.O. Box 9073
Boston, MA 02205-9948
U.S.A.

Royal Dutch Petroleum

Royal Dutch Petroleum is the majority partner (60 percent) in the Royal Dutch/Shell Group, the world's largest oil and gas conglomerate. It directly or indirectly owns shares in the group's holding companies, receives dividend income, and appoints the group's boards of directors. The group itself explores for and develops oil and natural-gas resources and operates in the businesses of chemicals, polymers, crop protection products, coal, and metals. Its chief operational subsidiary, Shell Oil, is one of the largest industrial corporations in the U.S., spending over $1 billion a year on oil-field exploration. This Dutch petrochemical titan has a strong commitment to the environment and a history of smart business decisions.

ROYAL DUTCH PETROLEUM (RD–NYSE) www.shell.com

Dividend Yield: 1.91%

Features of DRIP: Minimum initial investment of $250 and a $50 minimum for subsequent investments. Initial account set-up fee of $5. A $5 charge plus commission of 12 cents per share for each optional share purchase. Fee of $5 for sale of shares through the plan.

How to Contact: Morgan Guaranty Trust
P.O. Box 9073
Boston, MA 02205-9948
U.S.A.

British Airways

British Airways (BA) is one of the world's largest airlines. Based at London's Heathrow, the busiest airport in the world for international flights, BA serves over 170 destinations in more than 80 countries. About 20 percent of the company's revenues result from service to the Americas. BA has worked hard at upgrading its services and, through layoffs and restructurings, has transformed itself into a major player in the international airline market. The carrier has a 25 percent stake in my favourite airline, Australia-based Qantas Airways, which was made famous for its perfect safety record by Dustin Hoffman in the film *The Rain Man.* It is working to create alliances with other carriers, including American Airlines. BA is also starting a new, low-cost airline, Go, that will serve Europe. British Airways is a wonderful airline with a reasonable DRIP, and an excellent dividend rate.

BRITISH AIRWAYS (BAB–NYSE) www.britishairways.com

Dividend Yield: 7.15%

Features of DRIP: Minimum investment of $250, and a $50 minimum for optional cash purchases per month.

How to Contact: Morgan Guaranty Trust

P.O. Box 9073

Boston, MA 02205-9948

U.S.A.

Canon Inc.

Japanese manufacturer Canon is one of the world's top makers of business machines, cameras, and optical products, and the world's leading seller of cameras and colour copiers. Its major products include bubble-jet printers, laser printers, digital cameras, photocopiers, fax machines, single-lens reflex cameras, compact cameras, and 8 mm camcorders. Canon has developed ferroelectric liquid display technology for flat-panel, high-resolution display screens, which it expects to become the industry standard, replacing cathode-ray tubes in computer and TV screens. Canon has successfully increased its sales in the Americas and Europe and aims to boost revenues in the Asia/Pacific region outside of Japan.

CANON INC. (CAJ–NYSE) www.canon.com

Dividend Yield: 0.38%

Features of DRIP: Minimum initial investment of $250 and a $50 minimum for subsequent investments. Initial account set-up fee of $5. A $5 charge plus commission of 12 cents per share for each optional share purchase. Fee of $5 for sale of shares through the plan.

How to Contact: Morgan Guaranty Trust
P.O. Box 9073
Boston, MA 02205-9948
U.S.A.

These are ten companies I currently consider to be excellent investments. But the world is large! In the Appendix I have listed literally hundreds of other foreign companies in which you can participate directly. Use it as a starting point for the research that can lead to your own international investment adventure.

Chapter 9

DRIPS for My Kids and Yours

ONE FINAL AREA WHERE DRIPS CAN BE OF USE TO THE SMALL investor is as a first step in investing for kids. In this emergent — or rather resurgent — era of market-driven capitalism, it is likely a good idea for kids to learn about stock markets. When they reach the workforce they may even find that a portion of their income is in the form of stock options; this possibility alone is a solid argument for understanding markets. Their pension assets will almost certainly be heavily invested in equities — this is a second good reason for them to have insight into investing. Finally, the security of their employment may depend on the success in the investment world of the company they work for. All good reasons to consider getting your kids involved in investing — and what better way to do so than through the low-cost, long-term world of DRIPs?

MY CHILDREN'S DRIPS

My children, Riel and Geneviève, now 17 and 15, show little sustained interest in the world of investment to date. My advocacy of investing is no competition for the rhythms of their favourite rap singer or the latest Nike shoe. Despite their lack of enthusiasm, I have established several DRIPs in their names. They are modest, but with occasional cash contributions they will eventually provide an initiation for them into the world of investment. By the time the interest in rap music begins to fade, their curiosity about the economy and business may take hold. Eventually their need for a down payment on their first car or house may spark their interest, or, more likely, they may sell their DRIP shares and buy something frivolous just to annoy their father! Whichever route they choose, at least they will have some resources to fall back on.

In selecting DRIPs suitable for children, I stuck as a matter of convenience to ones I already owned. Partly I wanted names they might recognize from their purchase of products — Wendy's fit the bill. I also chose La-Z-Boy, to annoy my son, since his frenzied teen activity is the polar extreme to what is implied by the name of the famous recliner. I also included a stable, long-term utility in each of their portfolios. To date their holdings are tiny, but they're a start.

THEME-BASED DRIPS FOR KIDS

There is a wide variety of approaches to purchasing DRIPs for your children. One idea is to build a portfolio around a theme that interests the child. In the hope that you will have more luck convincing your children than I have had convincing mine, I've outlined some ideas for themes, beginning below the chart at the top of page 149.

Riel's DRIP Portfolio as of June 30, 2000			
Company	Shares Owned	Value	Business
Atmos Energy	11.4	U.S.$219	energy utility based in Texas
Johnson Controls	5.1	U.S.$268	auto parts; energy controls
La-Z-Boy Inc.	4.7	U.S.$70	furniture
Total: 21 shares		U.S.$557	

Geneviève's DRIP Portfolio as of June 30, 2000

Company	Shares Owned	Value	Business
Wendy's	16.2	U.S.$290	burgers and doughnuts
SBC Communications	2.7	U.S.$125	telecommunications
BC Gas	7.6	Can$145	gas utility
Total: 27.5 shares			**U.S.$560**

The Edible DRIP: The Way to Their Hearts Is Through Their Stomachs

You can construct an edible DRIP — one where all companies will appeal to your kids' stomachs. The recommended list would include McDonald's, Wendy's (which also owns Tim Hortons), Coca-Cola, Kellogg, Hershey Foods, Sara Lee, and PepsiCo. A few years ago an edible DRIP would have been able to include my own favourite, Dairy Queen. Unfortunately, Warren Buffett liked Dairy Queen so much that he bought the whole company.

The Toy DRIP: Play Is the Thing!

Another DRIP for kids could be built around toy companies, including Toys R Us, Mattel, Hasbro (makers of *Star Wars* toys), Sony, and others. Your children could conduct the key research at the local mall. Remember to set a budget, or after the mall you won't have any money left for the DRIPs!

An Entertaining DRIP

Another package of companies with kid appeal would include those that produce movies, theme parks, and music. Companies currently entertaining the kids include Walt Disney, Seagrams (PolyGram), CTV (now owned by BCE), Intrawest (ski resorts), and Alliance Atlantis (movies).

Clothing: Investments They Can Wear

Kids' clothing has spawned many lucrative businesses. Investment choices could include Gap, Tommy Hilfiger, Ralph Lauren (Polo), Suzy Shier (Wet Seal), Nike, and others. Again, a trip to the local mall could become a research expedition.

Sporting Equipment

Some sports have sparked the creation of whole companies that manufacture and market equipment for playing them. These companies include K2 (skis and snowboards) and Nike. Bombardier is a less focused investment — they make trains and planes as well as Sea-Doos.

Closer to Home: Basic Utilities

Although not as exciting as some of the other themes, a focus on the local electric, gas, water, and telephone companies could be educational. Your kids could learn about the companies that provide heat, light, water, and telephone service to your home. You could also include your bank (or theirs).

If you lived in Vancouver, British Columbia, the list would include BC Gas and Telus. If you lived in New York City, you'd buy Consolidated Edison and Bell Atlantic. In Calgary, Alberta, the telephone company would be Telus and the electric company could be TransAlta (both offer excellent DRIPs).

CAREFUL SELECTION

Of course, the idea of a theme for a children's DRIP does not remove the need for careful selection. You still need to review each company to make certain it is a solid, long-term investment. Fun is fine, but this needs to be a tad more serious. After all, money is involved — yours!

Many of the companies noted above are well known because they have built a strong brand name. Kids aren't the only ones who notice brands; the value of brand names in a global market is significant. A strong brand can be a clue to good investments. However, a brand name alone does not ensure a fundamentally strong company. You need to scrutinize the annual reports of would-be kids' DRIP companies to ensure growth, economic strength, and future prospects — as you would any other investment. Apply the basic rules discussed in Chapter 4. Are earnings well in excess of dividends? Are sales rising? Is there evidence of new products or services? All of these questions are worth considering. With sound research it is possible to lay a foundation for the financial security of your children. With luck, you may also teach them something useful about the economy.

OPENING THE DOORS OF COMMUNICATION

One way to engage your children is to obtain the annual reports of the companies you are considering. Share the reports with your children and let them choose. Not all annual reports are inspirational for children, but some will catch their interest. McDonald's, for example, has reports that are colourful and appealing.

A kids' DRIP portfolio affords an excellent opportunity to discuss investing with your children. The arrivals of the monthly and quarterly statements and of the annual report provide a good opportunity to talk. You can assign specific research tasks based on the reports received. For example, ask your child to find in the Wendy's annual report how many burgers the chain sold last year, from how many restaurants.

You could make share ownership more visible to your kids by purchasing a single, framed certificate from One Share of Stock Inc. (for more information, see Chapter 7). There are also a number of terrific Web sites described in Chapter 7 that can help teach kids about investments, for example, the Motley Fool and DRIP Central.

Of course, maybe the very fact that I am so enthusiastic about the investment world means that my children are unlikely to take an interest in it. Parents are never allowed to be cool in the minds of their daughters; isn't the cardinal rule that children may believe others to be cool, but never their parents?

I'll let Geneviève, whose questions started this book, have the last word. When I sought her advice on how to make a DRIP portfolio attractive to children, her first question, sensibly, was, "What is a portfolio?"

I explained, "A portfolio is just a fancy name for a group of stocks." Then I asked if she thought it was a good idea to build a child's DRIP portfolio around some themes.

She looked at me skeptically and pronounced, "Only if they are cool!"

Concluding Thoughts

GO INTO YOUR KITCHEN. GET YOUR LARGEST DRINKING GLASS and place it under your faucet. Set the tap to drip at as slow a pace as you can manage. Check back in a few hours, and your large glass will be overflowing. Why? DRIP . . . DRIP . . . DRIP . . . works!

I started this book by asking the question "Why one share at a time?" I hope to have made some progress in answering that question. If you have the courage to begin DRIP investing, I believe it will prove a worthwhile approach to creating a comfortable retirement for yourself. For $25 or $50 or $100 per month, you can begin a journey that has the potential to greatly assist your eventual retirement. This is a journey I have taken with considerable success and described in this book. I hope that in the previous pages you have found some inspiration, a road map, and some practical tools to aid your own journey.

Not that he would be considered a role model for investors, but the late and largely unlamented Chairman Mao commented wisely that a journey of a thousand miles begins with a single step. Don't delay in taking your first step on this journey. The first step of the Long March gained the Great Helmsman a nation. The first step of your journey can lead you to a more comfortable retirement.

The DRIP strategy has no barrier to entry — you don't need $20,000 or $50,000 or even $1,000. For as little as $25 you can buy one share of literally any one of hundreds of corporations. This single share is the first tiny step on a road to successful investment.

Remember that owning one share of a corporation opens the door to the most important privilege of being a shareholder — just as if you owned 1 million shares or 10 million shares: information. You have the right to attend the annual meeting and to vote for the board of directors. Most importantly, you are also entitled to receive the annual report and, if you wish, the quarterly reports to shareholders. My advice is to get them and read them.

As I confessed in Chapter 1, I did not start DRIP investing as an investment strategy. It was part of a research plan. But after I began to receive the monthly statements I realized that I could easily and cheaply add to my holdings of each company. I became a serious DRIP investor.

Owning a single share of a company with a DRIP can similarly open the door to further investment for you. One of the great features of DRIP investing is that it is habit forming.

A recent *New York Times* article was titled "DRIPs Aren't Sexy, and That's Their Charm." The author, Kate Berry, writes, "Dividend reinvestment plans can offer small investors, especially bargain hunters, an inexpensive way to buy shares." The real charm of DRIPs is that they actually work for investors, both small and large. If you want sexy, try a lingerie store or the Victoria's Secret catalogue. If you want a solid investment strategy, try DRIPs.

The approach outlined in this book builds upon my previous thinking in *Million-Dollar Strategy*. My investing philosophy and investment rules have not changed. The DRIP approach provides a road to be followed by would-be investors with small amounts of savings to begin to invest. With a DRIP strategy you build your own portfolio of investments in companies. And you can do it one share at a time.

The essential element in succeeding with a DRIP strategy is to begin. Having begun, you need to keep on, a little at a time.

Have an excellent DRIP adventure.

Appendix
More International DRIPs

Use this list as a starting point for research that may lead you to international investment adventures.

COMPANY	COUNTRY	BUSINESS	TICKER SYMBOL
ABN AMRO	Netherlands	banking	AAN
A financial holding company operating in some 70 countries.			
AEGON NV	Netherlands	insurance and finance	AEG
A worldwide insurance and financial services firm.			
APT Satellite Co.	China	satellites	ATS
Satellite-service provider for China and several other Asian-Pacific nations.			
Adecco	U.K.	employment services	ADECY
A temporary and permanent employment firm that operates in 30 countries.			
Aktiebolaget Electrolux	Sweden	appliances	ELUXY
Makes and sells household appliances.			
Akzo Nobel NV	Sweden	chemicals	AKZOY
Makes chemicals and pharmaceuticals products sold worldwide.			
Alcatel Alsthom	France	diversified	ALA
Operates in six business segments: telecommunications, cables, energy and transportation systems, batteries, and multimedia.			
Allied Irish Banks	Ireland	banking	AIB
Offers commercial and retail banking services in Ireland, the U.K., and the U.S.			
Amvescap PLC	U.K.	investment management	AVZ
Manages a wide range of portfolios for institutional investors.			

Amway Asia Pacific Ltd.	Asia	consumer products	AAP
Distributor for Amway Corporation's direct home sales in Asia.			
Amway Japan Ltd.	Japan	consumer products	AJL
Distributor for Amway Corporation's direct home sales in Japan.			
Aracruz Celulose SA	Brazil	paper products	ARA
Makes specialty paper products.			
Asia Pulp and Paper Co.	Singapore	paper products	PAP
Makes paper and packaging products.			
Astra A	Sweden	pharmaceuticals	AST.A
Researches and produces pharmaceutical products and advanced medical devices.			
Atlas Pacific Ltd.	Australia	minerals	APCFY
Owns South Sea Pearl farm and a majority interest in Forrest Belle/ Boudie Rat gold project in Western Australia.			
Banco Bhif	Chile	banking	BB
Offers a wide range of financial products and services to the retail and corporate banking markets in Chile.			
Banco Bilbao Vizcaye	Spain	banking	BBV
Conducts a retail banking business through 3,334 branches in Spain and 26 other countries.			
Banco Ganadero SA (common shares)	Colombia	banking	BGA
Provides commercial banking services to the domestic corporate, public, and retail sectors throughout Colombia.			
Banco Industrial Colombiano	Colombia	banking	CIB
Operates a general consumer and commercial banking service in Colombia.			
Banco Rio de la Plata SA	Argentina	banking	BRS
A private-sector commercial bank in Argentina.			
Banco Weise Ltdo.	Peru	banking	BWP
General banking business operating in Peru.			

Banco de Galicia y Buenos Aires	Argentina	banking	BGALY

Commercial bank based in Argentina, with branches in Uruguay and New York City.

Banco de Santander SA	Spain	banking	STD

Commercial and retail bank based in Spain, with over 500 foreign offices.

Banco de Santiago	Chile	banking	SAN

Operates a general commercial and consumer banking business in Chile.

Bank of Ireland	Ireland	banking	IRE

A leading Irish financial services group.

Bank of Tokyo-Mitsubishi	Japan	banking	MBK

A Japan-based bank that offers banking services worldwide.

Beijing Yanhua Petrochemical Co.	China	oil and gas	BYH

Manufactures and trades petrochemical products.

Benetton Group SPA	Italy	clothing	BNG

A maker of casual apparel for men, women, and children.

Blue Square-Israel Ltd.	Israel	retail	BSI

Operates supermarkets, department stores, and specialty stores offering a wide variety of products.

Boral Ltd.	Australia	diversified	BORAY

Makes building products and construction materials, provides a wide range of engineering services, and produces oil and gas.

British Petroleum Company PLC	U.K.	oil and gas	BP

Produces, transports, refines, and markets crude oil, natural gas, and related products.

British Telecommunications PLC	U.K.	telco	BTY

Provides local and long-distance telephone service in the United Kingdom.

CBT Group PLC	U.K.	software	CBTSY

Developer, publisher, and marketer of software titles covering a wide range of topics.

CLP Holdings Ltd. *China Light and Power Company.*	China	utility	CLPWY
CSR Limited *Producer of construction and mining products.*	Australia	mining; construction	CSRLY
Cadbury Schweppes PLC *Produces internationally branded chocolate and other confectionery products.*	U.K.	confectionery	CSG
Cantab Pharmaceuticals *Researches and develops proprietary biopharmaceuticals.*	U.K.	pharmaceuticals	CNTBY
Carlton Communications PLC *Film producer and maker of television, videocassette, and digital and analog products.*	U.K.	media	CCTVY
China Southern Airlines Co. *Provides airline services throughout China and Southeast Asia; operates the most extensive routes in China.*	China	airline	ZNH
Coca-Cola FEMSA SA de CV *Distributes, makes, and markets soft drink products of the Coca-Cola Company.*	Mexico	beverages	KOF
Companhia Brasileira de Distribucao *Operates home appliance stores and retail food stores in Brazil.*	Brazil	retail	CBD
Compania Cervecerias Unidas SA *Beermaker, bottler, and distributor in Argentina and Chile.*	Argentina/ Chile	brewing	CCUUY
Consorcio G Grupo Dina, SA de CV *Manufactures heavy-duty trucks and intricate buses.*	Mexico	motor vehicles	DIN
Corporacion Bancaria de Espana SA de Argentina *Bank based in Spain with nearly 100 foreign offices.*	Spain	banking	AGR

| Cresud | Argentina | agricultural products | CRESY |

Produces basic agricultural products.

| Dassault Systems | France | computers | DASTY |

Software developer for computer-aided design, manufacture, and engineering.

| De Rigo SPA | Italy | consumer products | DER |

Designs, makes, and sells premium sunglasses.

| Digitale Telekabel | Germany | cable television | DTAGY |

A German third-party cable television service provider to multifamily residences.

| Doncasters | U.K. | aerospace | DCS |

Makes engine parts for jet and turboprop airplanes worldwide.

| Durban Roodeport Deep Ltd. | South Africa | minerals | DROOY |

A medium-sized mining company that is a member of the Randgold & Exploration group.

| ELAN | Ireland | pharmaceuticals | ELN |

Worldwide company that develops drug-delivery systems.

| Empresas ICA SA de CV | Mexico | construction | ICA |

Constructs infrastructure projects, buildings, and residencies.

| Empresas La Moderna SA de CV | Mexico | diversified | ELM |

Cigarette maker and distributor of fresh produce and seed.

| Empresas Telex-Chile | Chile | telco | TL |

National telecommunications service provider in Chile.

| Esprit Telecom PLC | Europe | telco | ESPRY |

Telecommunications service provider with offices in the U.K., the Netherlands, Spain, France, Germany, and Belgium.

| FAI Insurances Ltd. | Australia | insurance | FAI |

Insurance company operating in Australia and New Zealand.

| FIAT SPA (ordinary shares) | Italy | motor vehicles | FIA |

Makes automobiles, commercial vehicles, and agricultural and construction equipment.

FIAT SPA (savings shares)	Italy	motor vehicles	FIA

Makes automobiles, commercial vehicles, and agricultural and construction equipment.

Fila	Italy	clothing	FLH

Manufactures athletic apparel and footwear.

Freepages Group PLC	U.K.	media	FREEY

Operates a classified information service for business, cinema, and film in the United Kingdom.

Fresenius	Germany	medical	FMS

Provides kidney dialysis services in 16 countries.

Gallaher Group PLC	U.K.	tobacco	GLH

Largest manufacturer of tobacco products in the United Kingdom.

General Cable	U.K.	telco	GCABY

Business and residential telecommunications services and cable television services in the United Kingdom.

Great Central Mines	Australia	minerals	GTCMY

Gold exploration in Western Australia.

Groupe AB	France	media	ABG

Television programming for French-speaking populations in over 45 countries.

Grupo Elektra	Mexico	household goods	EKT

Sells brand-name electrical appliances and furniture throughout Mexico.

Grupo Imsa	Mexico	metals	IMY

Processes steel; produces automotive and industrial batteries.

Grupo Industrial Durango SA de CV	Mexico	packaging	IMY

Manufactures packaging supplies in Mexico.

Grupo Iusacell SA de CV (series D)	Mexico	telco	CEL

Provides wireless cellular telephone services in Mexico City, Guadalajara, Puebla, Veracruz, Leon, Acapulco, and San Luis Potosi, Mexico.

Grupo Iusacell SA de CV (series L)	Mexico	telco	CEL

Provides wireless cellular telephone services in Mexico City, Guadalajara, Puebla, Veracruz, Leon, Acapulco, and San Luis Potosi, Mexico.

Grupo Tribasa SA de CV	Mexico	construction	GTR
Constructs infrastructure projects in Mexico.			

Guangshen Railway Co. Ltd.	China	railway	GSH
Operates railroad service in China between Guangzhou and Shenzhen.			

Harmony Gold Mining Co.	South Africa	mining	HGMCY
Mines for gold in South Africa.			

Huaneng Power International Inc.	China	utility	HNP
Constructs, owns, and operates coal-fired power plants throughout China.			

Huntington Life Sciences Group PLC	U.K.	research	HTD
Provides biological safety testing and research services to the pharmaceutical, agrochemical, and industrial chemical industries.			

INA	Italy	insurance	INZ
Life-insurance provider operating in Italy.			

IRSA	Argentina/Brazil	real estate	IRS
Real-estate developer for retail and office space in Argentina and Brazil.			

Imperial Chemical Industries	U.K.	chemicals	ICI
Produces special industrial chemicals.			

Industrias Bachoco SA de CV	Mexico	meat	IBA
Largest poultry producer in Mexico; also produces pork products.			

Industrie Natuzzi SPA	Italy	furniture	NTZ
Designs, makes, and sells leather and fabric-upholstered furniture.			

Ispat International NV	Netherlands	steel	IST
Owns and operates steel companies in Mexico, Trinidad, Germany, Canada, Tobago, and Ireland.			

Israel Land Development	Israel	diversified	ILDCY
Maintains a diversified portfolio of businesses.			

Istituto Mobiliare Italiano SPA	Italy	banking	IMI

Conducts a broad range of banking services based in Italy.

Jilin Chemical Industrial Co. Ltd.	China	chemicals	JCC

Produces basic raw materials and chemicals.

Koninklijke Ahold NV	Netherlands	food	AHO

Operates nearly 2,000 supermarkets and liquor stores in over 10 countries.

Koor Industries	Israel	diversified	KOR

Operates businesses in a variety of industries, focusing on telecommunications and electronics.

Korea Electric Power Corp.	Korea	utility	KEP

Operates the only utility generating electricity in South Korea.

Lihir Gold Ltd.	New Guinea	mining	LIHRY

Gold-mining project in New Guinea.

Lucas Variety PLC	U.K.	auto parts	LVA

Makes and supplies systems, products, and services for automotive and aerospace industries.

Luxottica Group SPA	Italy	consumer products	LUX

Makes high-quality eyeglass frames.

Maderas y Sinteticos	Chile	construction materials	MYS

Manufactures synthetic wood panels and doors.

Magyar Tavkozlesirt	Hungary	telco	MTA

Hungary's national telecommunications company.

Matsushita Electric Industrial	Japan	electronics	MC

One of the world's leading makers of electronic and electrical products for home, industrial, and commercial use.

Mavesa	Venezuela	food	MAV

Makes and sells a wide variety of food products.

Medeva PLC	U.K.	pharmaceuticals	MDV

Develops, manufactures, and sells a wide range of pharmaceutical products.

Mid-States PLC	U.K.	auto parts	MSADY

Distributor of automotive parts, mainly under the name Auto Value.

Modern Times Group AB	Sweden	media	MTGNY

Consists of a group of media companies that operate broadcasting, radio, publishing, electronic retailing, and media services businesses.

National Westminster Bank	U.K.	banking	NW

Retail bank in the United Kingdom with offices worldwide.

Nera AS	Norway	telco equipment	NERAY

Designs, makes, and sells telecommunications equipment.

New Holland NV	Netherlands	farm equipment	NH

Designs, makes, sells, and markets agricultural equipment.

New York Broker Deutschland	Germany	banking	NYBDY

Investment banking and market making firm.

Nippon Telephone and Telegraph	Japan	telco	NTT

Provides telecommunications services in Japan.

Norsk Hydro AS	Norway	chemicals	NHY

Produces and sells fertilizers and other chemical products.

Nortel Inversora SA	Argentina	telco	NTL

Telecommunications service provider in northern Argentina.

Novo Nordisk	Denmark	chemicals	NVO

Produces various biochemical products for use in medical treatments.

OzEMail Ltd.	Australia	Internet	OZEMY

Internet service provider in Australia and New Zealand.

PT Indosat	Indonesia	telco	IIT

Provides telecommunications services in Indonesia.

PT Inti Indorayon Utama	Indonesia	forest products	INRU

Makes and sells wood pulp for the paper industry and rayon fibre for the textile and garment industries.

PT Satellite Nusantara	Indonesia	satellites	PSNRY

A satellite-network development firm.

PT Telekomunikasi	Indonesia	telco	TLK

Operates the largest telecommunications concern in Indonesia.

Pacific Dunlop	Australia	consumer products	PDLPY
Makes a wide variety of consumer products.			
Petroleum Securities Australia Ltd. (Pestec)	Australia	oil and gas	PSALY
Conducts oil and natural-gas exploration in the Gulf of Mexico.			
Pfeiffer	Germany	equipment	PV
Designs and makes a wide variety of turbomolecular pumps and related components in over 33 countries.			
Pioneer Electric Corp.	Japan	electronics	PIO
Develops, manufactures, and markets electronic products.			
Pohang Iron and Steel Co. Ltd.	China	steel	PKX
Makes and sells a broad line of steel products.			
Portugal Telecom	Portugal	telco	PT
Portugal's national telephone company.			
Randgold & Exploration Co. Ltd.	South Africa	mining	RANGY
Gold exploration and mining.			
Repsol SA	Spain	oil and gas	REP
Explores and produces crude oil and natural gas.			
Ricoh Co. Ltd.	Japan	equipment	RICOY
Makes and distributes a wide range of business automation equipment.			
Rio Tinto Ltd.	U.K.	mining	RIO
Explores for mineral resources such as aluminium, coal, gold, iron ore, and copper.			
Royal Bank of Scotland (series B, C, D, E, F)	U.K.	banking	RBSB
Offers a wide range of banking services.			
Ryanair	U.K.	airline	RYAAY
Provides point-to-point flights between Ireland and the United Kingdom.			
SCOR	France	insurance	SCO
Insurance firm.			
SGS-Thomson	France	microelectronics	STM
Global independent semiconductor company.			

| Santos Ltd. | Australia | oil and gas | STOSY |

Explores for and produces oil and gas in Australia.

| Saville Systems Ltd. | Ireland | financial services | SAVLY |

Creates billing solutions for providers of global telecommunications services.

| Select Appointments (Holdings) PLC | U.K. | employment services | SELAY |

Provider of temporary and full-time staffing services to businesses.

| Select Software Tools PLC | U.K. | software | SLCTY |

Develops software tools used for analysis and design of application software.

| Senetek PLC | U.K. | biotechnology | SNTKY |

Sponsors biotechnology research.

| Shangdong Huaneng Power Development Co. Ltd. | China | electric utility | SH |

Owns interests in three coal-fired electric power plants in China.

| Shanghai Petrochemical | China | plastics | SHI |

Manufactures a wide range of synthetic fibres, resins, and plastics.

| Signet | U.K. | retail | SIGGY |

Operates a chain of jewellery stores in the United Kingdom and United States.

| Small World PLC | U.K. | software | SWLDY |

Software developer for complex engineering systems.

| SmithKline Beecham | U.K. | pharmaceuticals | SBH |

Develops, makes, and sells pharmaceutical products worldwide.

| TV Azteca | Mexico | media | TZA |

Holding company that operates Mexican television networks.

| Tag Heuer | Switzerland | watches | TWH |

Makes and sells sports watches.

| Telebras | Brazil | telco | TBR |

National telephone company in Brazil.

| Telecom Argentina | Argentina | telco | TEO |

National telephone company in Argentina.

Telecom Italia SPA (savings shares)	Italy	telco	TI

National telephone company in Italy.

Telefonica del Peru SA	Peru	telco	TDP

National telephone company in Peru.

Telefonos de Mexico	Mexico	telco	TMX

National telephone company in Mexico.

Thorn PLC	U.K.	rentals	THRNY

Provides a wide variety of goods through rent-to-own agreements.

Tubos de Acero de Mexico SA	Mexico	piping	TAM

Makes and sells piping products.

Unilever NV	U.K.	consumer goods	UN

Makes and markets a wide variety of consumer products.

Unilever PLC	U.K.	consumer goods	UL

Makes and markets a wide variety of consumer products.

Unionamerica Holdings PLC	U.K.	insurance	UA

Underwrites professional indemnity insurance.

Vimple Communications	Russia	telco	VIP

Telecommunications provider in Russia.

Vina Concha y Toro	Chile	beverages	VCO

Produces wine and other liquors for sale in Chile, and also exports fruit.

Vodafone Group PLC	U.K.	telecommuni-cations	VOD

Provides international mobile telecommunications services.

Waterford Wedgwood PLC	Ireland	ceramics and glass	WATFZ

Designs and makes a wide variety of china and crystal products.

Westpac Banking and Financial Corp.	Australia	banking	WBK

Operates a full-service bank in Australia.

The Wharf (Holdings) Ltd.	U.K.	investments	WARFY

Holding company whose subsidiaries own a wide range of investments such as property, hotels, infrastructure, tunnels, warehousing, and communications.

Xenova Group PLC	U.K.	pharmaceuticals	XNVAY

Specializes in the development of small-molecule drugs.

YPF SA	Argentina	oil and gas	YPF

Argentine oil and gas company.

Zeneca Group PLC	U.K.	pharmaceuticals	ZEN

Researches, develops, and makes ethical chemicals for agriculture and healthcare.

Useful Terms to Know

IN THE MYSTERIOUS WORLD OF INVESTING THERE ARE TERMS that can knock an amateur or new investor into the land of the confused. Here are a few definitions to help you avoid that uncomfortable journey.

AG
Allgemeine Gesellschaft or Aktiengesellschaft, a formal company designation used in Germany.

AMEX
American Stock Exchange. Based in New York, AMEX is the second largest floor-based exchange, after the NYSE. It has 661 members who transact trades in common shares and options on behalf of themselves and their clients.

BUY AND HOLD
an investment philosophy of buying stocks and holding them for the long term, typically 5 to 20 years.

CAPITAL GAINS
profits that come from selling shares at a higher price than their original cost.

CAPITAL LOSSES

losses that come from selling shares at a lower price than their original cost.

COST BASIS

the calculated cost of a particular share or group of shares of stock, necessary for calculating capital gains or losses.

CSA (CANADIAN SHAREOWNERS ASSOCIATION)

a Toronto-based association that provides information and services to its thousands of members, who are individual investors. You can join for a modest annual membership fee. Key benefits include a well-researched magazine and access to the Low Cost Investing Program. See Chapter 3 for more details.

DIVIDEND

a payment made to shareowners of a share of a company's profit, usually paid in cash on a quarterly basis. Some companies continue to pay dividends even when they are losing money. Some dividends are paid in shares.

DRIP (DIVIDEND REINVESTMENT PLAN)

a program offered by a publicly traded company in which dividends that are normally paid as cash to stockholders are used to purchase additional shares in that company.

DOLLAR-COST AVERAGING

a method of investing whereby an investor invests a specific dollar amount on a regular basis, such as monthly. When the share price is high, the value of all previously purchased shares goes up; when the share price goes down, there is an opportunity to purchase a larger number of shares at the lower share price. The advantage of this method is that an investor does not have to worry about "timing" the market.

MARKET TIMING

an attempt, usually futile, to time the best moments to get in and out of the stock market.

NAIC (NATIONAL ASSOCIATION OF INVESTORS CLUBS)

In the United States, investment clubs that pool together individual investors' monies are a broad phenomenon. This organization supports such clubs. See Chapter 3 for more details.

NASDAQ

National Association of Securities Dealers Automated Quotations, a U.S. electronic stock exchange.

NV

abbreviation for a formal company designation used in the Netherlands.

NYSE

New York Stock Exchange, the principal stock exchange in the United States.

OCP (OPTIONAL CASH PURCHASE)

a purchase of additional shares made through the dividend reinvestment account.

PLC

Public Limited Company, a formal company designation used in the United Kingdom.

PROCEEDS

the monies left after sale of shares and payment of fees and commissions, necessary to calculate capital gains and losses.

PT

abbreviation for a formal company designation used in Indonesia.

SA

Sociedad anonima, a formal company designation used in Spanish-speaking countries.

SHAREHOLDER OF RECORD

the owner of shares of a company's stock as registered in the company's files.

SIGNATURE MEDALLION GUARANTY

a formal program used by banks and other institutions to verify an individual's signature.

SPA

Società per Azione, a formal company designation used in Italy.

STREET NAME

a form of stock ownership in which shares are registered to a brokerage or other financial institution and held for the benefit of the firm's account holders.

TRANSFER AGENT

a financial institution or bank that manages the ownership records of a company's stock, including the transferral of any shares.

TSE

Toronto Stock Exchange, the principal stock exchange in Canada.

Index

ABN AMRO, 155
acquisitions. *See* takeovers
Adecco, 155
Advanced Micro Devices, 134
AEC Pipelines LP, 57. *See also* Alberta
    Energy Co.
AEGON NV, 155
aerospace, 159. *See also individual*
    companies
Aetna Inc., 131–32
AFLAC, 27–28, 33, 46, 88–90
AG Johansons Metallfabrik AB, 110
agricultural products, 159, 163
Aktiebolaget Electrolux, 155
Akzo Nobel NV, 155
Alberta, 48–49, 55, 58, 71, 150
Alberta Energy Co. (AEC), 55–57, 99
Alcatel Alsthom, 110, 155
Aliant Inc., 21–23, 67, 69–71
Alliance Atlantis, 150
Alliance pipeline, 56
Allied Irish Banks, 155
American Airlines, 144
American Association of Individual
    Investors (AAII), 122
American Drawing Rights (ADRs),
    135–37
Ameritech, 67
AMI Offshore, 70
Amvescap PLC, 155
Amway Ltd., 156
Anheuser-Busch, 125

annual reports. *See* reports
APM Inc., 131
APT Satellite Co., 155
Aracruz Celulose SA, 156
Argentina, 103, 156–59, 161, 163, 165,
    167
Asia, 156
    economy in, 60, 79
    immigration from, 48, 60
Asia Pulp and Paper Co., 156
assets, 38–39, 41
Astra, 156
Atlantic Canada, 69–71, 127
Atlas Pacific Ltd., 156
Atmos Energy Corp., 18, 107–8,
    129–30, 148
AT&T, 69
Australia, 66, 156–60, 163–66
automatic payments, 19
automotive industry, 78–79, 104
    outside North America, 158–60, 162

Banco Bhif, 156
Banco Bilbao Vizcaye, 156
Banco de Galicia y Buenos Aires, 157
Banco de Santander SA, 157
Banco de Santiago, 157
Banco Ganadero SA, 156
Banco Industrial Colombiano, 156
Banco Rio de la Plata SA, 156
Banco Weise Ltdo., 156
Bank of Ireland, 157

Bank of Montreal, 42, 126, 140
Bank of Tokyo-Mitsubishi, 157
banks, 50. *See also individual banks*;
    financial services
    consolidation of, 90–94
    DRIPs of, 123–24, 126
    as DRIP trustees, 18
    earnings of, 81–82
    outside North America, 155–58,
        162–64
Barbie, 132
Barclays Bank, 140
bargains, 40
Barings Bank, 139
Barrett, Matthew, 126, 140
Barron's Weekly, 73, 121
Bart, John, 34
Baryshnik, Jeff, 122
BCE Emergis Inc., 74. *See also*
    Bell Canada Enterprises Inc.
BC Gas Inc., 19, 28, 48, 60–61, 149, 150
BC Telecom, 48–49, 71
BCT-Telus Communications Inc.,
    71–72
Beijing Yanhua Petrochemical Co., 157
Bell Atlantic, 150
Bell Canada Enterprises Inc. (BCE),
    25–26, 67–68, 74, 150
Bell South, 42
Benetton Group SA, 157
Berry, Kate, 154
Better Investing, 35
beverages, 104, 158, 166
Bloomberg, 142
Blue Square-Israel Ltd., 157
Bombardier Inc., 75, 150
Boral Ltd., 157
brand names, 151
Brazil, 103, 156, 158, 161, 165
brewing. *See* beverages
Bre-X, 40
British Airways, 144
British Columbia, 28, 48–49, 60, 71
British Petroleum Co. PLC, 97, 157
British Telecommunications PLC, 157
brokers, stock, 9, 12, 85–86. *See also*
    commissions
    accounts with, 31

discount, 86
    and DRIPs, 113, 120–21
    on-line, 13
Bruncor Inc., 22–23, 69
Buffett, Warren, 2, 45–46, 90, 149
Burger King, 140
business magazines, 44
Business Week, 121
buy and hold, 45–46, 108
buybacks, 80, 96
*Buying Stocks without a Broker Using
    Dividend Reinvestment Plans*
    (Carlson), 122

Cadbury Schweppes PLC, 158
Caldwell Partners International, 124
Canadian Business, 121
Canadian General Investments Ltd.
    (CGI), 72–77
Canadian Hunter, 55
Canadian Mainline, 64
Canadian National Railways, 23
Canadian Pacific Ltd., 77–78
Canadian Shareowner, 34
Canadian Shareowners Association
    (CSA), 27, 34–35, 115
Canon Inc., 144–45
Cantab Pharmaceuticals, 158
capital gains tax, 23, 24–25
Carlson, Charles B., 122
Carlton Communications PLC, 158
cash investment option, 18–19, 30
CBT Group PLC, 157
CDNX exchange, 123
Celestica Inc., 75
chemicals, 155, 161–63. *See also*
    oil and gas
Chernow, Ron, 97
Chevron, 97
Cheyenne Light, Fuel and Power Co.,
    100
Chile, 156–59, 162, 166
Chilton, David, 17
China, 109, 155, 157–58, 161–62,
    164–65
China Southern Airlines Co., 158
Chips & Technology, 134
Chrysler, 11

CIBC, 126
CIBC World Markets Inc., 79
Cisco, 68
clothing, 150, 157, 160
CLP Holdings Ltd., 158
CMP Group Inc., 23
CNBC, 39
Coca-Cola, 149, 158
Colombia, 103, 156
commissions, 13, 85–86, 113, 137.
    See also fees
Companhia Brasileira de Distribucao, 158
Compania Cervecerias Unidas SA, 158
companies
    American, 85–88, 129–35
    Canadian, 53–54, 85, 123–29
    choosing for DRIPs, 20–21, 28–29, 38, 41–42, 47, 88, 150–51
    comparing, 30
    lower risk, 11, 43, 46
    monitoring, 31
    number to invest in, 29–30
    outside North America, 135–45, 155–67
    researching, 7, 30–31, 38–39
Comper, Tony, 126
competition, 100. *See also* mergers; regulation
computers, 104, 159
connectors, 109
Consolidated Edison, 150
consolidation
    in financial services sector, 88, 126
    in telecommunications industry, 100
    of water utilities, 107
Consorcio G Grupo Dina SA de CV, 158
construction, 158–59, 161–62
consumer products, 156, 159, 162, 164–66
Consumers Water Co., 105–6
convergence, 67
Coors, 125
Corporacion Bancaria de Espana SA de Argentina, 158
cost base, 24–25, 45
Cresud, 159

CSR Ltd., 158
CT Financial Services Inc., 74
CTV Network, 67, 150
Cyrix, 134

Dairy Queen, 149
Dassault Systems, 159
Dayton Hudson, 130
day trading, 13
decision-making, 45
Decter, Geneviève. *See* Roch-Decter, Geneviève
Decter, Riel. *See* Roch-Decter, Riel
defence, 109
Denmark, 163
De Rigo SPA, 159
Diageo PLC, 140–41
Digitale Telekabel, 159
digital revolution, 26, 47, 66
Direct Investing, 121
direct purchase plans (DPPs), 2
direct stock purchase (DSP), 120
discount brokers, 86
discounts
    on dividend reinvestment, 19
    on share purchases, 17, 73, 86
Disney. *See* Walt Disney Co.
diversification, 21, 25, 29–30
dividend reinvestment plans (DRIPs).
    See also fees
    American, 85–88, 129–35
    basics of, 2, 5
    benefits to company of, 8
    benefits to investor of, 8–11, 25
    Canadian, 51–53, 85, 123–29
    choosing companies for, 20–21, 28–29, 38, 41–42, 47, 88, 150–51
    closing of, 23
    companies offering, 11
    drawbacks of, 11–12
    funds for, 10
    inherited, 25
    as investment strategy, 16
    minimum and maximum investments in, 19
    outside North America, 135–45, 155–67
    publications about, 121–22

and risk, 11, 25
starting, 9, 10
and taxes, 24–25
theme-based, 148–50
dividends
converting to income, 33
defined, 5–6
taxes on, 24
Dofasco Inc., 53, 78–80
dollar-cost averaging, 10
Doncasters, 159
DoSol Galva, 78–79
Dow Jones Indexes, 53
Dow Jones Sustainability Group Index
(DJSGI), 53–54, 65–66
DRIP. *See* dividend reinvestment plans
DRIP Advisor, 120
DRIP Central, 8, 114, 138, 151
*The DRIP Central Guide to DRIP
Investing* (Gerlach), 122
The DRIP Drop, 120
DRIP Investing, Step by Step (Gerlach),
122
DRIP Investor, 122
"DRIPs Aren't Sexy, and That's Their
Charm" (Berry), 154
Durban Roodeport Deep Ltd., 159

earnings growth, 20
e-commerce, 69
Edward Jones Water Utility Index, 106
ELAN, 159
electricity. *See* utilities
Electrolux, 155
electronics, 162, 164
employment services, 124, 155, 165
Empresas ICA SA de CV, 159
Empresas La Moderna SA de CV, 159
Empresas Telex-Chile, 159
Enbridge Inc., 28, 53, 62–63
energy, 64–65. *See also* oil and gas;
utilities
Energy East Corp., 23
energy royalty trusts, 55, 58–60
Enermark Income Fund, 59–60
Enerplus Resources Fund, 59–60
Enron, 104, 107
entertainment, 133, 149–50

e prime, 100
Ericsson, 110
Esprit Telecom PLC, 159
Esso, 58
Evergreen Enterprises, 122
Exxon Mobil, 58, 97–99
Exxon Valdez, 99

FAI Insurances Ltd., 159
Falconbridge Ltd., 75
Fannie Mae, 131
*Fee-Free Investing: How to buy stocks
and bonds and never pay a broker's
fee* (Baryshnik), 122
fees, 137–38. *See also* commissions
brokers', 9
for cash investment, 19, 85–86, 137
for dividend reinvestment, 17, 18,
138
set-up, 9, 19, 137
of shareholders' associations, 34, 35
withdrawal, 9, 19
FIAT SPA, 159–60
Fidelity Magellan, 38
Fila, 160
files. *See* research
Financial Post, 121
financial services, 82. *See also* banks
consolidation of, 88
outside North America, 155–58,
165–66
Finland, 142
First Marathon, 82
First Share Cooperative, 121
Fisher, George, 116
food industry, 94–97
outside North America, 158, 161, 162
Forbes, 121
Ford Motor Company, 6, 24, 28,
134–35
forms
S-3, 8
T-5, 24
1099, 24
Fortune, 121
France, 155, 159, 160, 164
Freepages Group PLC, 160
Fresenius, 160

Frith Brothers Investments, 116
funds
    closed-end equity, 72–73, 76–77
    managers of, 42–43
    mutual, 42–43, 73

gains. *See* capital gains
Gallaher Group PLC, 160
Gap, 150
General Cable, 160
Gerlach, Douglas, 122
Germany, 159, 160, 163, 164
*Global Investing 1999: A Guide to the 50
    Best Stocks in the World* (Leckey),
    89
Globe and Mail, 67, 121
Go airline, 144
goal setting, 32–34
Goulds Pumps, 109
government regulation, 64–65, 82
Grand Metropolitan PLC, 140
Gray, James, 55
Great Central Mines, 160
Groupe AB, 160
growth
    of companies, 46–47
    of earnings, 20
Grupo Elektra, 160
Grupo Imsa, 160
Grupo Industrial Durango SA de CV,
    160
Grupo Iusacell SA de CV, 160
Grupo Tribasa SA de CV, 161
Guangshen Railway Co. Ltd., 161
Guinness, 140

Häagen-Dazs, 140
Hard Rock Cafe, 140
Harmony Gold Mining Co., 161
Hasbro, 149
Hershey Foods, 149
Hong Kong, 48, 71
Horton, Tim, 96
household goods, 155, 160, 161
Houston Industries. *See* Reliant Energy
    Inc.
Huaneng Power International Inc., 161
Hungary, 162

Huntington Bancshares, 90–92
Huntington Life Sciences Group PLC,
    161

IBM, 19, 33, 110–11
Illinois Central Railway, 23
iMagicTV, 70
immigration, 48, 60, 71
Imperial Chemical Industries, 161
Imperial Oil, 41–42, 55, 58, 99
INA, 161
income, 33
indexes. *See* stock indexes
*The Individual Investor's Guide to
    Dividend Reinvestment Plans*
    (AAII), 122
Indonesia, 163
Industrias Bachoco SA de CV, 161
Industrie Natuzzi SPA, 161
industries, 44, 45. *See also specific
    industries*
inflation, 102
InfoInterActive, 70
infoMarket, 111
information, company, 7, 43–44, 154.
    *See also individual Web sites and
    publications*; Internet; research
information technology, 69–70, 162
ING Groep NV, 139–40
innovation, 70–71
insurance, 88–89, 159, 161, 164, 166.
    *See also individual insurance
    companies*
Intel, 104, 133–34
interest rates, 49
Internet
    as business, 67, 104, 163
    buying DRIPs on, 6, 113–14
    and e-commerce, 69
    as research tool, 39, 42, 44
    as source of DRIP information, 6, 7,
        95
Intrawest, 150
investing, 9–10, 16, 29. *See also specific
    types of investments*; fees
Investing for Dummies (Tyson), 122
investment clubs, 85
investors, 13

investors' associations, 34–36. *See also*
   individual associations
IPL Energy Inc. *See* Enbridge Inc.
IP products, 68. *See also* technology
IPSCO Inc., 127
Ireland, 155, 157, 159, 165, 166
IRSA, 161
Island Tel Advanced Solutions, 69–70
Island Telecom Inc., 69
Ispat International NV, 161
Israel, 157, 161, 162
Israel Land Development, 161
Istituto Mobiliare Italiano SPA, 162
Italy, 157, 159–60, 161, 162, 165
ITT Industries, 18, 108–10

Japan, 88–89, 138, 156, 157, 162–64
JDS Uniphase Canada Ltd., 74
Jilin Chemical Industrial Co. Ltd.,
   162
Johnson Controls, 148
Joyce, Ron, 96
J.P. Morgan, 119, 136

K2, 150
Kaman Sciences, 109
Kellogg, 149
Kmart, 130
Koninklijke Ahold NV, 162
Koor Industries, 162
Korea Electric Power Corp., 162

Labatt, 124–25
La-Z-Boy, 148
LCIPs (low-cost investing programs).
   See individual shareholders'
   associations
Leckey, Andrew, 89
Leeson, Nick, 139
Lévesque Beaubien Geoffrion, 82
liabilities, 39
Lihir Gold Ltd., 162
losses. *See* taxes
Lotus, 111
Lucas Variety PLC, 162
Lucent, 68
Luxottica Group SPA, 162
Lynch, Peter, 38, 42–43, 131

Maderas y Sineticos, 162
Magyar Tavkozlesirt, 162
Mao Zedong, 153
Maritime Telegraph and Telephone
   Co. Ltd., 69
market. *See* stock markets
Mark Resources, 59
Matsushita Electric Industrial, 162
Mattel, 132, 149
Mavesa, 162
Mayberry, John, 79
McDade, Douglas C., 22–23
McDonald's, 15–16, 18, 19, 94–95, 149,
   151
Medeva PLC, 162
media, 158, 159, 160, 163, 165.
   See also individual companies;
   telecommunications
medical services, 160
mergers, 12. *See also* takeovers
   of banks, 126
   effect on DRIPs of, 21–24, 45
   in financial sector, 82, 90–94
   in oil and gas industry, 98
   in steel industry, 79
   of stock exchanges, 123
   in telecommunications, 71–72, 100
   of utilities, 101–2, 105–6
Mexico, 158–61, 165, 166
Michael Decter's Million-Dollar
   Strategy, 1, 7, 17, 20, 37, 154
microchips, 104
MicroInvestor Web Guide, 117
Mid-States PLC, 162
Miller Brewing, 125
mining, 123, 158–62, 164
Mining Co., 117
MITI Information Technology Inc.,
   69–70
Mobil, 33. *See also* Exxon Mobil
Modern Times Group AB, 163
Molson Inc., 124–25
Money, 122
Montreal Stock Exchange, 123
Morgan, Gwyn, 56–57
Morito, Akio, 138
The Motley Fool, 117, 151
Motorola, 110

National Association of Investors
    Clubs (NAIC), 35–36, 115
National Bank of Canada, 80–82, 126
National Post, 73, 121
National Westminster Bank, 163
Natural Fuels, 100
natural gas, 53, 56. *See also* pipelines;
    utilities
NBTel, 69–70
Nera AS, 163
Netherlands, 155, 161–63
Netstock, 119–20
New Century Energies, 49, 100–103
New Century International, 100
New Guinea, 162
New Holland NV, 163
NewTelk Enterprises Ltd., 69
New York Broker Deutschland, 163
New York Stock Exchange, 137
New Zealand, 66
next-generation networks (NGNs), 68
Nike, 150
Nippon Telephone and Telegraph,
    163
Nokia, 110, 142
NorAm, 103
Norsk Hydro AS, 163
Nortel Inversora SA, 163
Nortel Networks Corp., 16, 46, 68–69,
    74
Northern States Power, 49, 101–2
Northwest Territories, 58
Norway, 163
NOVA, 64, 83
NOVA Chemicals Corp., 83–84
Nova-Net Communications, 70
Nova Scotia Power, 127
Novo Nordisk, 163

oil and gas, 53, 54–66
    dividends from, 123
    outside North America, 157, 164,
    165, 167
O'Neill, Dan, 125
One Share of Stock Inc., 115, 151
OPEC, 54–55
open-market purchase, 18
OzEMail Ltd., 163

Pacific Dunlop, 164
packaging, 160
paper, 156
P&C (personal and commercial)
    bank earnings, 81–82
pensions, 8
PepsiCo, 149
performance, 30, 32
Periphonics, 69
Peru, 156, 166
petrochemicals. *See* oil and gas
Petroleum Securities Australia Ltd.
    (Pestec), 164
Pfeiffer, 164
pharmaceuticals, 156, 158–59, 162,
    165, 167
Philadelphia Suburban Corp., 105–7
Pillsbury, 140
Pioneer Electric Corp., 164
pipelines, 53, 56, 60, 64, 70, 83, 127.
    See also individual companies
piping, 166
plastics, 165
PMC-Sierra Inc., 75
Pohang Iron and Steel Co. Ltd., 164
Polo (Ralph Lauren), 150
PolyGram, 150
population growth, 71
portfolio, 152
    diversifying, 21
    tracking, 31–32
Portugal Telecom, 164
Power Investing with DRIPs, 116–17
price, 12
profits, 39
proxy ballots, 31
PT Indosat, 163
PT Inti Indorayon Utama, 163
PT Satellite Nusantara, 163
PT Telekomunikasi, 163
The Public Register, 120
Public Service Company of Colorado,
    49–50, 100
pumps, 109, 164

Qantas Airways, 144
quarterly reports. *See reports*
Quebec, 81

Quicken, 12
Quixx, 100

Ralph Lauren, 150
Randgold & Exploration Co. Ltd., 164
Rank Group PLY, 140
real estate, 161
record keeping, 11–12, 24–25, 30–31, 45
Registered Retirement Savings Plan (RRSP), 1, 33, 60
regulation
  in energy sector, 64–65
  in financial sector, 82
REI Trading and Transportation, 103
Reliant Energy Inc., 103
rentals, 166
Report on Business, 121
reports
  analysts', 32
  company, 31, 154
  ordering, 31
  as research tool, 38–39, 41, 44, 151
Repsol SA, 164
research, 30–31, 38–39, 43–45, 151
resource industries, 128, 156, 163.
  See also mining; oil and gas
retail sector, 157, 158, 165
retirement planning, 4, 7–8, 33–34.
  See also Registered Retirement
  Savings Plan
returns, 25–26
Reuters, 142–43
Ricoh Co. Ltd., 164
Rio Tinto Ltd., 164
risk, 11, 25, 29
Roch-Decter, Geneviève, 5–6, 15–16, 27, 147–49, 152
Roch-Decter, Riel, 147–49
Rockefeller, John D., 97
Royal Bank of Canada, 28
Royal Bank of Scotland, 164
Royal Dutch Petroleum, 143
Royal Trust, 11
royalty trusts, 55
RRSP. *See* Registered Retirement
  Savings Plan
Rule Industries Inc., 110

Russia, 166
Ryanair, 164

Salter Street Films, 70
Sampson, Anthony, 97
Santos Ltd., 165
Sara Lee, 149
satellite communications, 70, 155, 163
Saville Systems Ltd., 165
savings
  converting to income, 33
  as discipline, 17, 32
  DRIPs as vehicle for, 9–10, 24
SBC Communications, 149
SCOR, 164
Scotiabank, 126
Sea-Doo, 150
Seagrams, 150
Securities and Exchange Commission (SEC), 8
Seely, Jeff, 119–20
Select Appointments (Holdings) PLC, 165
Select Software Tools PLC, 165
Senetek PLC, 165
separatism, 81
*The Seven Sisters: The Great Oil
  Companies and the World They
  Made* (Sampson), 97
SGS-Thomson, 164
Shangdong Huaneng Power
  Development Co. Ltd., 165
Shanghai Petrochemical, 165
shareholders rights, 7, 31, 154
shareowners' associations, 85, 113, 115–16. *See also individual
  associations*
share-price appreciation, 28, 50
share purchase plans (SRPs), 2
shares. *See also* discounts
  buybacks of, 80, 96
  buying, 12, 17, 18, 45
  new issue, 18
  selling, 6, 12, 45, 138
  value of, 21–22
Shell Oil, 143
Signet, 165
Singapore, 156

Sinopec, 109
Sinton Engineering Group, 110
Small World PLC, 165
Smirnoff, 140
SmithKline Beecham, 165
soft drinks. *See* beverages
software, financial, 12
software industry, 104, 157, 165
Software Kinetics Ltd., 70
Sollac, 78
Sony, 28, 138–39, 149
Sorbo, Anna, 79
South Africa, 159, 161, 164
South Korea, 162
Southwestern Public Service Co., 100
S&P 500, 106
space station, 109
Spain, 156, 157, 158, 164
Standard Oil, 97
statements, investment
    filing, 11–12, 45
    ordering, 31
    as research tool, 28–39, 30, 32, 151
steel, 53, 79, 160, 161, 164
stock exchanges. *See individual
    exchanges*
stock indexes, 73. *See also individual
    stock indexes*
stock markets
    analysis of, 38–39, 47–48
    volatility of, 43
stock splits, 16
Stratos Global Corp., 70
Suez Lyonnaise des Eaux, 104
Suncor Energy, 53
sustainability, 53–54
Sustainable Asset Management, 53
Suzy Shier, 150
Sweden, 155, 156, 163
switches, 109
Switzerland, 165
Syncrude, 55
Synovus Financial Corp., 92–94

Tag Heuer, 165
takeovers, 12. *See also* mergers
    of water utilities, 104, 105–6
Target stores, 130

tariffs, 79
taxes, 23, 24–25
    importance of records for, 11–12, 45
technology, information, 69–70, 162
technology sector, 11, 162, 164, 165
Telebras, 165
Telecom Argentina, 165
Telecom Italia SPA, 166
telecommunications, 99–100, 155.
        See also individual companies;
        utilities, telephone
    outside North America, 157, 159,
        160, 162–66
Tele-Direct, 67
Telefonica del Peru SA, 166
Telefonos de Mexico, 166
telephone companies. *See* utilities,
    telephone
Telus, 48–49, 67, 71–72, 150
Temper Enrollment Service, 120–21
1099 forms, 24
Texas, 103, 107–8
T-5 forms, 24
Thomas, Dave, 96
Thorn PLC, 166
Tim Hortons, 96–97, 149
Titan (Chernow), 97
tobacco, 160
Tommy Hilfiger, 150
Toronto Dominion Bank, 75
Toronto Stock Exchange, 63, 79, 123
Toys R Us, 149
track record, 46–47
Traders Building Association, 41
TransAlta Corp., 42, 48, 53, 65–66, 150
TransCanada PipeLines, 19, 48, 63–65,
    83
transfer agents, 12, 34
transportation, 158, 161, 164. *See also
    individual companies*
trends, 40, 47–50, 88
trust companies, 18, 34
trustees, 18
trusts, 128–29
    energy, 55, 58–60
    royalty, 55
TSE 300, 63
Tubos de Acero de Mexico SA, 166

TV Azteca, 165
Tyson, Eric, 122

Unilever, 166
Unionamerica Holdings PLC, 166
United Kingdom, 155, 157–67
USA Today, 122
Usinor Group, 78–79
US West, 69
utilities, 99–103, 148, 150. *See also*
    individual companies
  DRIPs of, 123–24
  electric, 28, 29, 47, 49–50, 53, 100
  and inflation, 102
  natural gas, 48, 54–55
  outside North America, 158, 161,
    162, 165
  telephone, 25–26, 28, 47, 48, 66–72
  water, 104–7
Utility Engineering, 100

value, 38–39, 41
Vancouver Stock Exchange, 123
Venezuela, 162
Vimple Communications, 166
Vina Concha y Toro, 166
Visteon, 24
Vodafone Group PLC, 166
volatility, 43
voting, 31, 154
VSAT data networks, 70

Wall Street Journal, 121
Wal-Mart Stores Inc., 130
Walt Disney Co., 133, 150
water. *See* utilities, water
Waterford Wedgwood PLC, 166
Watson, John, 57
The Wealthy Barber (Chilton), 17
Web sites, 44
  for DRIP resources, 113–20, 151
Wendy's, 96–97, 148, 149
WestGas Interstate Inc., 100
Westpac Banking and Financial Corp.,
    166
Wet Seal, 150
The Wharf (Holdings) Ltd., 167
wine. *See* beverages
Winnipeg Stock Exchange, 41
Worth, 42–43

Xcel Energy Inc., 49–50, 100–103
Xenova Group PLC, 167
xwave solutions inc., 69

Yahoo! Finance, 7, 12, 31–32, 44,
    117–18
Yellow Pages, 67
yield, 32, 49
Yorkshire Electricity Group PLC, 100
YPF SA, 167

Zeneca Group PLC, 167